Art and Worship

The new Alcuin Liturgy Guides series revives the tradition of the Alcuin Manual. The Guides are essentially concerned with the practice of liturgy, its setting and celebration. The aim is to publish two Liturgy Guides in alternate years, following the publication of books of liturgical scholarship and commentary, the so-called Alcuin Collection.

The projected topics for the new Liturgy Guides series include the celebration of the Eucharist; children, communion and confirmation; music in worship; and the use of liturgical symbols in worship. The majority of these titles will consider the new rites and services of *Common Worship*, and together will, to all intents, form a third volume of the *Companion to Common Worship*. The series editor is the Revd Christopher Irvine.

Members of the Alcuin Club receive free copies of the Collection, Liturgy Guides, and the Joint Liturgical Studies. The Alcuin Club promotes the study of Christian liturgy, especially the liturgy of the Anglican Communion, and its chairman is Dr Donald Gray CBE. Details of membership may be obtained from the Revd Tim Barker, The Parsonage, 8 Church Street, Spalding, Lincolnshire PE11 2PB.

Art and Worship

Anne Dawtry and Christopher Irvine

Alcuin Liturgy Guides 2

Published in Great Britain 2002 by
Society for Promoting Christian Knowledge
Holy Trinity Church
Marylebone Road
London NW1 4DU

British Library Cataloguing-in-Publication Data
A catalogue record for this book is available from the British Library

ISBN 0–281–05425–8

Typeset by Wilmaset Ltd, Birkenhead, Wirral
Printed in Great Britain by
Antony Rowe Ltd, Chippenham, Wiltshire

Contents

Introduction: Looking and Seeing

This book is a manual, a small book to hold in the hand, to guide the reader as he, or she, looks at the terrain of art and worship. First we shall raise the issues which have featured in discussion of the place of art in churches, look at how we *see* art in churches, and then consider how we might heighten our sensitivity to the artistic dimension of worship. It is essentially a practical book, a book to assist the reader to appreciate the many ways in which visual and plastic arts might work in a place of worship. But why this renewed interest in art? The answers to this question are manifold.

Gone, it seems, are the days when art was for the privileged connoisseurs. Groups of local people and their children from the surrounding housing estates gather under the towering figure of Antony Gormley's *Angel of the North,* which proudly stands above the post-industrial Tyneside town of Gateshead. Crowds, much larger than were expected, daily visit the recently opened Tate Modern Gallery on Bankside in London, and the National Gallery's millennium exhibition *Seeing Salvation,* with its accompanying television series and publications, was an unanticipated phenomenal success. Cultural and social commentators might well ask what is happening. It is a cliché to observe that we are living in a visual age. We are constantly bombarded with images on advertising hoardings, television and video. At every turn we are confronted with images, images deliberately designed to draw our attention, to beguile, and to persuade us to get more and to spend more. No one can doubt the power of images. A visual culture seeks to catch the eye, a designer world which audaciously says, 'Look at this', or more precociously, 'Look at me!' No wonder then, that we have become voyeuristic in our viewing. We look in on other people's lives, and on our roads and in our city-centres the ubiquitous CCTV cameras remind us that we too are being looked at.

But why does art draw such numbers? Is it that having had our eyes opened, we recognize the need to learn to look, our deep human need to catch a vision? Are we compelled to look for something to kindle our imagination, for something to give clarity to our confusions, and to give form to our hopes and aspirations? Images can convey religious truth, art can suggest, challenge and pose the deepest questions of life.

Art can open up for us the very question of God, of our values and meaning. Works of art, such as a Vermeer painting of a domestic scene, or a Matisse still-life, can help us to look beyond ourselves, help us to see the real world, and focus our eyes on the objective world, a world 'out there'. Art can also make visible the invisible, it can open up other possible worlds, and mediate the very life of God. For pictorial art has often expressed and communicated Christian doctrine, by giving visible form to that divine self-communication, which theologians call 'revelation'. Religious art can be profoundly theological. One might think, for example of Botticelli's *Mystic Nativity,* a picture of the birth of Christ, which shows that event as the hinge of history, the turning of the ages, with the banishing of the destructive forces of evil, and the angelic celebration of the new order of peace. The intricate and delicate paintings of David Jones include subtle and symbolic images which need to be 'read', not just seen, but really looked at.

The surge of interest in art is also seen in the academy, and recently a number of academic theologians have found in art a rich resource for theological reflection and for speaking of God's relation with the created order. One of the most notable publications in this regard has been John Drury's *Painting the Word: Christian Pictures and Their Meanings* (1999), a sumptuously illustrated book, which provides a theological exposition of some of the religious paintings in the collection of the National Gallery in London.

Much religious art of the past was not painted to be hung in galleries, but was commissioned for churches. What the art shows, and how it works, is of course related to this context. What we *see* in a piece of art is, in many ways, determined by the setting, architecture and ambience of *where* it is seen. Thus in Chapter 1 we give a summary of some of the issues which have emerged in the theological discussions and controversies concerning the place of art within the Church. Here, theological convictions are tied to history, and the story is spelt out further in Chapter 2. One of the aims of this present book is to encourage the dialogue between artists and the churches, and in Chapters 3 and 4 we indicate the kind of conversations which need to be had between artists and the Church. These chapters take a practical look at how we might view religious art in places of worship, and although some of the examples cited are concentrated within a particular geographical area, the points that are drawn out from our chosen examples are of general significance and application regarding the placing of art in churches. Churches, of course, are primarily places of prayer, and the question of how art works in relation to the work of worship is a continuous thread through the book and receives explicit treatment in Chapter 5. The placing of art and the reordering of churches has serious legal ramifications, and these are fully set out in the final chapter. As one would rightly expect with a manual or guide, we are concerned with the promotion of good practice, and the book concludes with a directory listing organizations and agencies which can offer professional advice, inspiration and support.

But perhaps one real and pressing issue remains to be addressed, and that is finance. It seems as though many churches have been living beyond their financial means, and monetary constraints pinch tighter as congregations age and shrink. This, we are told, is the inexorable effect of secularization in western societies. But perhaps the Church has too readily colluded and even connived with the myth of secularism. There is a greater interest and good will towards the Church than we might imagine, and a church building is valued by many who would rarely cross the threshold. For many of the so-called uncommitted appreciate that a church building is a sign of the transcendent, and if approached, might well be willing to contribute financially to its upkeep, care and beautification. Our Victorian forebears were adept at building new churches through public subscription, but generally, these new places of worship were rarely, if ever, full on a Sunday morning. We need to be pragmatic, but not lose sight of the poetic and prophetic, the need for communities to have their sacred places, markers, and focal points. So the religious needs and sensibilities of 'non-churchgoers' in the wider community should not be overlooked. But perhaps above all, all of us need art in churches, to create, as that great twentieth-century prophet of church art, Fr Marie-Alain Couturier OP said, 'places of enchantment, poetry and deliverance' ('Aunque es de noche', Couturier, 1989, p. 105).

Chapter 1

The Theological Agenda for Art and the Church

The use of art as a means of enhancing the place of worship has been part of the Christian tradition ever since early believers took it upon themselves to decorate the walls of the catacombs with Christian symbols and images relating to the Christian story of salvation. Yet theologically down the centuries the use of art in churches and within worship has raised just as many questions as it has answered. For example, should Christian art, much of which has been figurative, be encouraged because it enhances our understanding of the Godhead, or be discouraged on the grounds that, since we can never know what God looks like, then we should not try to represent him lest we mislead the worshipper?

Another debate has centred around the relationship of Christian art to the word of God. In the time of the Church Fathers, Gregory the Great saw art as the picture book of the people. Yet Calvin and other Reformation thinkers regarded representational art as unnecessary to the people if they were being adequately informed by the preaching of the word which painted its own pictures for the Christian soul.

Finally, while theology clearly does influence art, affecting the types of images of God and the saints which have been portrayed down the centuries, one must also ask the question as to whether art, as von Balthasar argues, can also influence theology and indeed provide for us a whole new system for doing theology differently from those theologies we have hitherto encountered? David Brown has recently worked along this axis, and has argued that through art the Christian imagination has enlarged our apprehension of Christian truth (Brown, 1999 and 2000). If art is a medium for the unfolding of revelation, then one might ask which criteria one might employ to evaluate the claimed truth of what is given and shown. The questions we have alluded to are not the only questions one might wish to ask. Yet within the scope of this work these questions are perhaps sufficient to make the point that in the relationship between art and worship and between art and theology there have always been paradigms, differently expressed at different times, but always with the same suspicion asking whether or not there is within the Christian tradition an essential tension between art and worship.

The origin of this conflict goes back beyond Christianity to the Judaic traditions of the Old Testament. At first glance we find a contradiction here between Exodus 20.4–5 and Deuteronomy 4.15–16, on the one hand, where making any graven image is forbidden and Exodus 25.18–20 where it is God himself who orders Moses to have images of the cherubim crafted for the tabernacle. Again while the prophets of the eighth century BCE protested against cultic images and denounced them as idols (Isaiah 2.8; Hosea 13.2), and the psalmist mocked them as empty 'no-gods' (Psalm 135.15ff.), it is clear that art played an important part in the construction of the temple of Solomon (or more possibly in the construction of the second temple in Jerusalem) as described in 1 Kings 7.13–14 and 2 Chronicles 2.13–14. The aesthetic impact of the temple court is also attested to in a number of the psalms as in Psalm 27.6; 50.2; 65.4; 84. What is going on here? Were there really two traditions in complete conflict with one another within Judaism, one (the Deuteronomic) with an almost iconoclastic hatred of images and the other, which Walter Brueggemann calls the 'tabernacle tradition' (Exodus 25–31; 35–40), believing that God's awesome presence was palpable in the visual splendour of the temple (Brueggemann, 1997, pp. 425–30)? Was the one tradition, that in which images were used, earlier than the tradition which forbade them? Certainly many Jewish scholars have seen it this way. Yet if this was the case then it would hardly account for the lavish decoration of the second or third temples which postdated the Deuteronomic prohibition or for the decoration of synagogues such as that discovered at Dura Europas and described in Chapter 2.

A more likely explanation is that the prohibition was never intended to be a universal one. It is more likely that the prohibition against the making of 'graven images' originally referred to sculptured forms, or to forms of God himself who cannot be seen yet is to be adored. This did not prevent the use of other decorative art in synagogue and temple for enhancing the place of worship. Portrayal of angelic beings such as were made for the tabernacle would probably be acceptable in this schema since angels were messengers from God to humanity and as such had been seen by human eyes. This compromise allowed a thoroughly Hebrew aesthetic to surface which is woven into the narrative framework of Hebrew scriptures and is seen as a gift of God. In this the very ability of the artist and craftsman to design and decorate the temple was attributed to the inspiration of the Spirit (Exodus 35.31). Similarly, the later Wisdom tradition sees the creative energies of God as not only pervading the whole universe, but as being brought to expression in the work of those skilled in design, art and craft. It was they who maintained the fabric of the world, and whose prayer was in the practice of their craft (Sirach 38.34). Recently this theme has been taken up by Aída Besançon Spencer when she argues: 'The Bible is a wonderful apologetic for art since it shows God as the master artist who creates works of art that art is a natural part of life and an effective means of enhancing God's work. Furthermore because God created human beings we inherit from God the capacity to subcreate and symbolise' (Spencer, 1988, p. 26).

The conflict between art and theology did not arise within Christianity until the debate over icons in the eighth century CE and then only in the eastern Church. In the West the suggestion of Gregory the Great that sacred art was to be encouraged since it provided a picture book for the illiterate was generally accepted (*Epistle* 2.13, cited in Walker, 1996, p. 19). The debate within Orthodoxy centred around whether it was legitimate or not to create images of Christ and the saints and whether these images or icons thus created were suitable objects for veneration. The Iconoclasts (726–835), who called for a banning of all such images and for their wholesale destruction, seem in some ways to have been affected by a form of the dualist thinking which had plagued Christianity from its earliest centuries. This Gnosticism places matter and spirit in direct opposition to one another and as such has a tendency to subvert the very logic of the incarnation. The Iconoclasts argued that since Christ and the saints were no longer on earth, then they must not be represented in icons since to do so in some way denied that they were now part of the spiritual realm and lessened both the divinity of Christ and the sanctity of the saints. Yet it cannot be doubted that they were also almost certainly moved by asceticism and by a strong moralism which said that the money used to produce the icons would be better spent on the poor.

Against the Iconoclasts the Iconophiles, or supporters of icons (chief among them John Damascene) argued that icons were important because they drew the believer nearer to the invisible Christ. In his *Oratio* John Damascene argued that although human beings had no direct knowledge of divine figures, nor of the events of their lives from which they were separated by time and space, yet, when a person viewed a representation of Christ or one of the saints then there was in some sense a lapse of distance between the worshipper and the subject of the icon. It was as if the viewer were standing before the depicted event, or figure, who according to iconic conventions faced, and therefore engaged, the viewer. He stated furthermore that while it would be wrong to make an image of the invisible God yet since Christ had been made human he had opened himself up to being known and represented. Indeed for Damascene icon painting and the use of the icon in worship were a justifiable means of contact with the incarnate Christ and his saints. If, he said, the invisible Word had taken flesh (John 1.14) and had appeared in human form (Philippians 2.7) as the visible image of the invisible God (Colossians 1.15; 2 Corinthians 4.4b) then makers of Christian art, even though conscious of the risks of misrepresenting God and of misleading the worshipper, took risks in making an image in human form precisely because it was in that human form in which the incarnate Christ had been made manifest in the historical Jesus. Furthermore, the very use of physical materials, the wooden boards, fabrics, paint, glass and marble, were seen as a witness to the mystery of the incarnation, the epiphany of the divine life in the very material of creation.

John Damascene also made a distinction between worship of the icon itself and of the Godhead which it represents:

> Now that God has appeared in the flesh and lived among us, I make an image of the God who can be seen. I do not venerate matter, but I venerate the Creator of matter, who for my sake became material and deigned to dwell in matter, and who through matter effected my salvation . . . matter filled with divine power and grace. (*On the Holy Icons* 1.16)

Following this principle he clarified the difference between worshipping icons and venerating them (the word 'venerate' means literally 'to embrace and to kiss lovingly'). This distinction was to form the basis of the ruling of the Third Ecumenical Council of Nicaea in 787 on icons and Damascene's writings, especially the *Apologia*, have formed the basis of the eastern Churches' justification for icons ever since.

Such a viewpoint, however, can only be justified when, as Basil of Caesarea famously put it, the honour and veneration of Christian images is directed to the archetype, that is, the transcendental reality which they represent. Yet even such a neat caveat, as Christian history will show, did not always provide a foolproof safeguard against a superstitious view and use of religious pictures, images and objects. The human psyche seems to need its talismans, and this has been a perennial danger for those who would make and appreciate religious art.

In the twelfth-century Church of western Christendom the paradigm between art and theology appeared again in a different guise. This time the issue was whether the use of images or decoration in churches enhanced worship or whether it distracted the eye and the concentration of the worshipper away from God present at the altar in the Eucharist in the form of bread and wine. It is probably no coincidence that this debate, in which the main protagonists were Abbot Suger (1081–1151), builder of the Abbey of St Denis near Paris, and Bernard of Clairvaux (1091–1153), the most influential Cistercian of his day, took place at a time when veneration for the Eucharist was growing in western Christendom. Suger, fragments of whose stained glass from St Denis, rescued at the time of the French Revolution, can still be found at Wilton in Wiltshire, at Twycross in Leicestershire and at Castle Raby in County Durham, saw the art and architecture of the Church as a vehicle for experiencing the inestimable beauty of God and as a means of participating in the life of God. His beautifully decorated abbey church at St Denis was designed to translate worshippers in their devotions to the heavenly city. As they passed through scenes of the Last Judgement at the entrance the pilgrims would have been conscious of passing over a threshold into a new kind of relationship with God. From here they looked towards the east end, bathed in light from its many stained glass windows, and gazed at the many wonders of the abbey church, which served as a reminder of the heavenly city to which they aspired. (For more on Suger and the Abbey of St Denis, see Panofsky, 1946.) Against the mysticism of Suger and of the Benedictines Bernard of Clairvaux and the Cistercians took a different view. Bernard saw religious art and decoration as distracting the worshipper from concentrating on God and on the centrality of the Eucharist. (On the Cistercian view of aesthetics and the decoration of their abbey churches, see Chapter 3.)

The debate on whether art distracted the worshipper or not grew ever more fierce in the sixteenth and seventeenth centuries. This was the age of Renaissance and Reformation. In the Catholic Church creativity took on a new lease of life and the artist rose from being simply the maker to being in a co-creative relationship with God. New baroque masterpieces were created with images of Christ, Mary and the saints, together with leagues of supporting angels. The Roman Catholic Church defended this work on the grounds that showing reverence to religious paintings and images was not idolatry, since theologically honour was being shown not to the images themselves but to the proto-types or realities which those images represented. Moreover the Roman Catholic hierarchy believed that such images continued to have an important educational purpose in calling to mind biblical events and Christian doctrines in the hearts of those who gazed on these images (*Canons and Decrees*, 1848, pp. 1233–36).

Yet already at the end of the fourteenth century another contrary view-point was making itself heard. In his treatise on the Decalogue, *Tractatus de mandatis divinis* (1375–76), John Wyclif set out his ambivalence to the gallery of medieval religious art and warned his readers how any lingering of the eye on an image could all too easily lead to idolatry. Such views one might expect to have been endorsed wholeheartedly by the major figures of the Reformation, by Luther and Calvin on the continent, and by Thomas Cranmer in England. Yet this was not entirely the case. In Germany Martin Luther defended ecclesiastical art in terms of its didactic purpose. He spoke of images as 'enhancing the word': 'I do not think it wrong to paint such stories along with verses on walls of rooms and chambers so that one might have God's words and deeds constantly in view' (Luther, *Works*, vol. 43, p. 43). He also included painting in a list of the ways in which God's word can be effectively communicated (Luther, *Works*, vol. 13, p. 168). To this end he himself patronized artists and engravers to further his own theological agenda, among them Albrecht Dürer and Lucas Cranach. Luther however did insist that the use of art must always be an external sign purposed to enhance the word. While he condemned the iconoclasm of other reformers such as Karlstadt on the grounds that they prevented Christian freedom, Luther himself was uncomfortable with the presence of images in churches especially those visited by pilgrims as a means of salvation by works. This is hardly surprising given Luther's own stance on justification by faith alone.

John Calvin, the main figure in the second generation of reformers, was more robust in his opposition to images than Luther had been. In his *Institutes of the Christian Religion* he states that giving form to God, any form, was a corruption of God's glory since it was inevitably the object which ended in being worshipped rather than God himself (*Institutes* I.xi.2). He believed that sculpture and painting should be confined to representing those things which the eye was capable of seeing. 'Let not God's majesty which is far beyond the perception of the eye be debased through unseemly representations' (*Institutes* I.xi.12). He included within his prohibition not only images of the saints but images of Christ on the grounds that in recounting the ascension, scripture stresses 'the withdrawal of Christ from our thinking carnally of him so that when we recall him our minds may be raised up to seeking him in heaven' (*Institutes* IV.xvii.36). Calvin also objected to the teaching of Gregory the Great that images were the books of the unlettered on the grounds that if the Church had been preaching the word properly then these images would not have been needed in the first place (*Institutes* I.xi.7).

However, as a reformer of the second generation Calvin had learned much from the excesses of the Iconoclasts of the first. Thus he refused to be gripped by the sort of superstition which denounced all art and images on the grounds of the prohibition in Exodus 20. Instead he was willing to see both painting and sculpture as God's gifts for which we must find a pure and legitimate use for God's glory rather than misusing and polluting these gifts to our own destruction (*Institutes* I.xi.12). Tantalizingly, however, Calvin never elaborates on what he sees as a pure and legitimate use of these gifts as he is more concerned with how they can be used to humanity's destruction.

The same ambivalence to the place of art in the Christian scheme of things outlined by Luther and Calvin on the continent was also discernible in the English Reformation. Thomas Cranmer was himself unconvinced by Luther's moderate view and use of religious art. Already by 1530, aesthetically blinkered, perhaps, and fearful of the dangers of idolatry, he ventured the opinion: 'I think it more convenient for Christian religion that images should be taken out of men's churches, than that they should be placed in the temple of God' (Aston, 1988, p. 432). His own personal views did not change over time but were unequivocally expressed again in the address he gave at the coronation of the boy king, Edward, on Sunday, 20 February 1547: 'Your majesty is God's vice-regent and Christ's vicar within your own dominions, and to see with your predecessor Josiah, God truly worshipped, and idolatry destroyed, the tyranny of the bishops of Rome banished from your subjects and images removed' (Cranmer, 1848, p. 127).

In the early 1530s there was a wave of iconoclasm in the south-east of England and again in a more widespread fashion at the dissolution of the monasteries between 1536 and 1540. In this latter, under the supervision of Thomas Cromwell, the demolition and removal of cultic objects – rood screens, statues, crucifixes was virtually wholesale. Yet unlike Cranmer, Cromwell and those employed to strip the monasteries were not moved by ideology or of religious scruple, but were encouraged instead by monetary incentive and sometimes by the thrill of performing acts of vandalism in the name of the law.

Henry VIII although supporting the dissolution of the monasteries for financial reasons attempted to dampen the zeal of the Iconoclasts, issuing a letter banning the contentious preaching of the radicals in January 1536. It is also almost certain that the Ten Articles, issued by the bishops in the summer of 1536, which offered a qualified affirmation of images in churches, had the support of the king. In the Articles images were seen to be 'representers of virtue and good example . . . the kindlers and firers of men's minds especially the images of Christ and our Lady'. Yet although the sixth Article affirmed that images 'should stand in the church', the emphasis was placed on the need for preachers to warn the 'rude people' against acts of superstition and alert them to the dangers of idolatry. The so-called 'Bishops' Book' (*The Institution of a Christian Man*) in 1537, made this more explicit:

> we are utterly forbidden to make or have any similitude or image, to the intent to bow down to it, or worship it. And therefore we think it convenient that all bishops and preachers shall instruct and teach the people . . . that God in his substance cannot by any similitude or image be represented or expressed.

An even more lenient view towards the visual apparatus of Catholic worship was shown in the so-called 'King's Book' (*A Necessary Doctrine and Erudition for any Christian Man*), published in 1543. Although the book followed the Protestant rendering of the second commandment, it stated that the prohibition against images was not a blanket prohibition of all images, but of those which were idolatrously abused:

> We are not forbidden to make or to have similitudes or images, but only we are forbidden to have them to the intent to do godly honour to them . . . And therefore, although images of Christ and his saints be the works of men's hands only, yet they be not so prohibited but that they be had and set up both in churches and other places.

Elizabeth I, like her father, also showed some latitude in her attitude towards church ornaments and vestments and this enraged some of the more puritanical bishops of her day, like John Jewel, recently returned from Geneva. In 1559 Bishop Jewel wrote to his reformer friend Peter Martyr that 'doctrine is everywhere most pure; but as to ceremonies and maskings there is a little too much foolery. That little silver cross of ill omened origin still retains its place in the Queen's chapel' (Loades, 1979, p. 255). Yet after more than two decades of religious and political controversy Elizabeth I was above all pragmatic and followed in her policies about religion what was expedient rather than any consistent religious ideology.

It was during Elizabeth I's reign that Richard Hooker completed the task of writing what was to become the definitive apologia of the English Church, the *Laws of Ecclesiastical Polity*. In this work he set out to show how the very constitution of the Church of England was in accordance with divine law. Hooker has been credited with setting out the basis for what has become known as the Anglican *via media*, which has been misconceived as a compromised fudge but was the precise orientation of the worship and ecclesial self-understanding of the English Church between reformed Geneva and Catholic Rome. In Book V, published in 1597, Hooker affirmed the church building as a 'sacred space' in fulsome prose:

> The very majesty and holiness of the place where God is worshipped hath in regard of us great virtue, force and efficacy, for that it serveth as a sensible help to stir up devotion, and in that respect no doubt bettereth even our holiest and best actions of this kind. (*Laws*, V.vvi.2)

A sense of this same *via media* was celebrated by the seventeenth-century priest-poet, George Herbert (1593–1633), in his poems posthumously published under the title *The Temple*. In 'The Church Porch' Herbert celebrates the *via media* of the English, between the visual austerity of the Calvinist conventicle and the garishly decorated Roman churches. His love for the Church was shown in his care for the church building, which he regarded as the meeting place of God and the individual soul: 'When once thy foot enters the church, be bare. God is more there than thou'. His sense of the importance of ordered liturgical worship alongside preaching, was demonstrated in his arrangements for the refurbishment of the parish church at Leighton Bromswold, where two pulpits, both of the same height and dimensions, one for preaching, and the other for the leading of corporate prayer, were situated on either side of the chancel arch, thus showing an equal balance between preaching of the word and public liturgical prayer.

Despite this restoration of the church building and all that was in it as a holy space in the thought of Hooker and Herbert, in the age of the Industrial Revolution of the eighteenth and nineteenth centuries art to a large extent parted company from religion. It began instead to have a rationale and an aesthetic entirely separate from that of the Church. The human being became a creator in his own right rather than being a maker, with God as Creator (as the artist had been seen in the Middle Ages), or a co-creator with God (as the artist had been understood at the Reformation). As Goethe wrote in 1804, 'art has consolidated its status as an independent cult sometimes more flourishing than that of the churches themselves' (Ford, 1997, p. 672). Art also began to be seen as intended for human pleasure and recreation (William Morris) rather than for the glory of God (Osborne, 1997, p. 80). This shift in the equation had its effect on both the Church and the art world simultaneously. As the twentieth century dawned art was becoming increasingly individualistic and autobiographical often with no communal, let alone liturgical, imperative for the use of the Bible as a point of departure for inspiration. The artistic quest for spiritual meaning – for the truth beyond what we see – was now often completely independent of, and sometimes in direct conflict with, the milieu of established religion. From the Church's perspective fewer great artists were now commissioned to create works of art in churches than ever before which had the effect of damaging still further the dialogue between art and the Church.

Despite this changed relationship between artists and the Church, however, a number of theologians have continued to discuss the relationship between religion and art in their work, thus keeping alive the hope that the debate between artists and the church may be far from dead. These theologians have by and large fallen into three categories which John Dillenberger has described thus (John Dillenberger, 1986, pp. 15–28). First, there are those theologians who see no relationship between the arts and theology in their work. Second, there are those theologians who see a positive relationship between theology and the arts which they have sometimes been able to articulate successfully and sometimes not. And third, there are those theologians who have allowed the arts to speak to them in such a way that they provide paradigms and images which have affected the whole nature of their theological method.

Dillenberger sees the chief figure in his first category as being the theologian Karl Barth. Yet this is only true in relationship to the visual arts and within the context of church worship. Barth's claim that images and symbols have no place in a building designed for Protestant worship seems unequivocal (Ford, 1997, p. 677). In this Barth is being true to his roots within continental Protestantism, shared by Bultmann, in which the Word is paramount. Yet Barth also suggests that art outside worship can witness to the truth of the revelation of God in Jesus Christ as in the case of the figure of John the Baptist in Grünewald's Isenheim altarpiece which had deeply moved him on a personal level. And in the case of the other arts, especially music, Barth was far from willing to exclude the connection between art and divine revelation (Ford, 1997, p. 690). A composition by Mozart, he wrote, is not only something beautiful if it is played well but also takes on something of the quality of a parable about the kingdom of God. Thus Barth does not, we would argue, fit into the first category as neatly as might be at first supposed but contains within his theology a personal paradigm in which his Protestant background is combined, especially in the musical sphere, with a deeply aesthetic self.

Into Dillenberger's second category fall a number of theologians some of whom such as Rahner and Tillich he lists, others like Rudolf Otto in Germany and Percy Dearmer in England whom he does not. Dearmer (1867–1936) was vicar of St Mary's, Primrose Hill and later a canon of Westminster Abbey. In his writing on art and religion published during the First World War he proposed that God was revealed in the three transcendentals of goodness, truth and beauty. The task of the theologian he argues is to articulate the truth of beauty, while the challenge to the artist was not self-expression but to bring the beauty of God to expression. So far so good, but such convictions required a more systematic elucidation than Dearmer was capable of giving and thus according to Dillenberger's second category Dearmer would have been only partially successful. Perhaps more successful in elucidating the beautiful and the holy was the German theologian Rudolf Otto. In his seminal work *The Idea of the Holy* (1959) he draws a comparison between the religious experience of the numinous and the aesthetic experience of the beautiful. Otto believed in the power of the abstract to convey the numinous experience and thus opened up the possibility for the use of abstract art within worship. Yet unfortunately for the scope of the present work, he does not consider it part of his brief or purpose to develop how this might be achieved in practice.

Karl Rahner and Paul Tillich concentrate in their writings not so much on the contemplation of beauty but on the place that the arts hold in theology. Rahner in an important but neglected essay discusses the relationship of the arts to the verbal arts that in preaching and in the proclamation of the word have held sway in western Protestant theology since the Reformation. He argues for a new place to be found for the visual and performing arts alongside the verbal arts on the grounds that these arts are also expressions of human transcendence and openness to the revelation of the divine mystery (Rahner, 1982, pp. 24–25.) Paul Tillich is rather more ambitious. In his writings he sets out to prove that there was no area of human life with which theology was not concerned, and that the arts, lamentably ignored in Protestantism, raised the deep questions of human existence which only the divine could answer. On the basis of this method of correlation between the human and the divine, Tillich argued that art could be expressive of the divine, and concluded that some art was religious in style, but not in subject matter, while some was religious in subject matter but not in style (Apostolos-Cappadona, 1996, p. 311). This posed the question, still debated within the Church today, as to whether art in churches must be of an explicit religious subject, and indeed, of whether it needs to be the work of a Christian artist. Yet Tillich's work is limited in that despite his avowed purpose, he never develops a systematic analysis of the relationship between theology and the arts. Instead his main work in this sphere *On Art and Architecture* comprises a number of studies on individual works of art in an attempt to show how these works can be interpreted as expressions of ultimate concern.

An attempt to publish a systematic study of theology and art, which does its theology through art rather than vice versa (Dillenberger's third category), finally came to fruition in the work of Hans Urs von Balthasar. Entitled *Herrlichkeit* or *Glory* this work in seven volumes, which he began to publish in 1961, is original not only in its ambition but also in its method. The work is aesthetics read theologically and goes far beyond merely pointing out Christian themes in works of arts or in drawing parallels between theology and painting. It is a monumental work of theological construction. He says comparatively little about works of art themselves, but sets out to argue how God's beauty is revealed in the form of Jesus Christ. In this way von Balthasar aims to construct a whole new approach to theology in which he begins by comparing the Christian faith with aesthetic enjoyment. Yet he moves far beyond the mere interplay in our consciousness of subject and object in the aesthetic mode to revelation as object i.e. as art. Our consciousness receives revelation in the way that a drama or a mosaic mirrors subjectivity; the people and events in God's reign appear in a pattern similar to the way artworks enter our mind and emotions. This is not to imply that revelation is a symbol rather than a reality, but that the reality of Jesus Christ was both hidden and disclosed, and that the Kingdom of God, preached by Jesus, employs a variety of forms to exist around and within us as something to be both believed and encountered (Apostolos-Cappadona, 1996, p. 212).

Von Balthasar shows that aesthetics draws on what is first a contemplative stance which is prepared to accord a primacy to object and which respects the integrity of the form which is perceived, letting the form of the object discipline and condition its responses. In the same way in theology, he argues, in attending to form the contemplative person receives revelation, not as a mirror reflects an image, but by a kind of imaginative participation. The object of contemplation thus generates life beyond itself. In the same way the response of the contemplator can be a medium by which that which is contemplated is also transposed, or transfigured.

Von Balthasar's *Glory* is by far the most detailed and systematic work of theological aesthetics which has been attempted. Yet interest in this field and in the whole relationship between art and theology is far from dead today and looks set to continue well into the twenty-first century. Among other recent works worth mentioning are Richard Harries, *Art and the Beauty of God* (1993), J. Begbie, ed., *Beholding the Glory* (2000), D. Apostolos-Cappadona, ed., *Art, Creativity and the Sacred* (1996), and the scholarly work of R. Viladesau, *Theological Aesthetics* (1999), which examines the role of the imagination in theology and seeks to elucidate the relationship between beauty and the sacred. Harries, on the basis of a biblical faith, makes the case for an aesthetical theology, while Begbie and Apostolos-Cappadona adopt a more interdisciplinary approach. Begbie's book examines the incarnation from the perspective of literature, poetry, dance and music, sculpture and icons, while *Art, Creativity and the Sacred* brings together contributions from artists and art historians as well as from theologians and philosophers. It is this interdisciplinary approach which perhaps above all gives hope that the dialogue between artists and the Church has once more arisen like a phoenix from the ashes as a new dialogical community, a reflection of our life in Trinity, in which conversation, undistorted communication and communal judgement can both inform and transform our lives in the world (Begbie, 1992, p. 79). It is this dialogue which will be explored further in later chapters.

Chapter 2

A Brief History of Art in Church

Christianity took root in a largely pagan environment, in the cities of the Roman empire, and its practitioners would have been familiar with the riches of Greco-Roman art and architecture. Yet like the Jews of the diaspora, the first urban Christians struggled to safeguard a vision of the transcendent God in a social world which was furnished with the visual apparatus of pagan worship: statues, altars and temples of the gods. They needed to preserve their distinctive identity and to keep their vision of God undefiled by pagan practices, even to the point of death. The second-century Alexandrian theologian Origen was unequivocal on the matter:

> Christians and Jews are led to avoid temples and altars and images by the command . . . You shall not make a carved image for yourself nor the likeness of anything in the heavens above, or in the earth below, or in the waters under the earth. You shall not bow down to them or worship them. (*Against Celsus* VII.64)

Similar directives are found in the writings of Tertullian, who saw a risk in admitting painters and craftsmen into the community of faith since their work could easily bring them into contact with pagan artefacts and religious objects (*De Idol.* VIII.1–2). This fear of contamination was real, and echoed St Paul's repeated injunction to refrain from idols. Behind it was an overriding concern to maintain the social identity and religious cohesion of the Christian community as the 'new Israel'.

Maintaining a sense of identity inevitably depends upon the assertion of difference, and Christians, unlike their pagan counterparts, were not to live in a world furnished with religious images and artefacts. Hence the polemically charged character of early Christian apologetic. But as Mary Charles Murray argued in a seminal article on art in the early Church, we must also be cautious of reading into the literary evidence a general hostility to art per se (Murray, 1977). Indeed, once Christians were more secure in their social setting, free from persecution, and afforded the legal status of a public cult in the fourth century, there was an apparent change of attitude towards the place of visual arts and artefacts in their homes and places of worship. However, this burgeoning of Christian art cannot be accounted for solely in terms of changing social and political factors and circumstances. There was something inherent in the developing Christian self-understanding which led to its artistic expression in line, form and colour. Perhaps it was a logical outcome that visual signs, figures and forms came to be drawn from the scriptures with their rich texture of imaginative and figurative language. Nevertheless, there is a considerable tension in holding together the view of God as Creator with an appreciation of the human being as a maker, and this tension has resulted in recurrent episodes of iconoclasm throughout Christian history.

During such periods the Old Testament law was read as a strict prohibition against the making of images. But was this intended as a universal prohibition? As we have already seen in Chapter 1 the prohibition against the making of 'graven images' originally referred to sculptured forms of God himself. And in the Jewish tradition this tradition was set against another, equally powerful one in which it was understood that God's awesome presence was palpable in the visual splendour of the temple. There is also archaeological evidence of Jewish representational art, which if not technically 'narrative art', depicts scriptural events and figures. Admittedly the earliest surviving examples to be found in the Jewish catacombs, or burial chambers in Rome date from the mid-second century CE, but there is no reason to suppose that these are not part of an already well-established tradition. Here, discovered in the mid-nineteenth century, were wall paintings, and funerary art, including sculptured figures and engraved stone surfaces. Another striking example of Jewish representational art was in the synagogue at Dura Europas which, when it was excavated in the late 1920s, was found to have been richly painted. Other examples witness to the development of other art in Jewish circles, such as the use of mosaics in the sixth-century synagogue at Beit Alpha, located below Mount Tabor.

Some of the earliest art in a place of Christian worship to have been discovered is that from the church-house at Dura Europas adapted for liturgical need in about 240 CE. Excavated between 1930 and 1934, the church-house at Dura Europas was in a unique location, at a crossroads of culture, which over the centuries had been home to a variety of peoples of different religious traditions and affiliations. The church-house was one of a number of dwellings on the periphery of the town later filled with rubble and sand to widen the town's fortifications. The building, typical of its kind, consisted of eight rooms surrounding an open courtyard. A dividing wall between two of the rooms was removed to create a room which could accommodate up to 60 people, making an assembly room where in all likelihood the community gathered for the celebration of the Eucharist. Another room was adapted for use as a baptistery. Here a range of artistic decoration has survived, now to be seen in the University of Yale Art Gallery.

We can only imagine the impact that this room would have had upon a candidate for baptism. At one end was a large baptismal basin, over which was constructed a decorated canopy supported by two frontal pillars. The front-facing rim of the arch was decorated emblematically with alternating ears of wheat and grapes, recalling the Eucharist, while the underside, above the basin, was decorated with stars against a dark blue background. On the rear wall was painted the figure of the Good Shepherd, bearing the Christian soul to the 'good pastures', where they might be nourished for eternal life. Smaller figures of Adam and Eve, possibly painted later, were positioned below the representation of the Good Shepherd, possibly to indicate the call of Christ to the whole of humanity to enter into the fullness of life. The universality of Christ's call, however, is balanced also by a consideration of the particular, especially for those who would step into the baptismal font and be drawn up into the Christian community, on the other side. For in the immediate foreground there is an empty space, a space in which, as it were, the individual who emerged from the water of baptism could picture themselves being called and led by Christ. Around this space, on two bands around the walls, were a series of paintings, sketchy and impressionistic in style, representing selected scriptural events from both the Gospels and the Hebrew scriptures. As they are positioned, the figures literally face the viewer, and thereby almost demand a response to the meanings which they evoke and express. Like the other decoration of the baptistery they are integral to what was being ritually enacted in the way in which they give vital visual form to the meaning of baptism.

Similarly, we might consider the art of the Christian catacombs in Rome, where members of the community would lay their beloved departed to rest in the hope of the resurrection. The earliest of these catacombs were contemporary with, and some even pre-date, the church-house in Dura, and the frescoes, painted directly onto the plaster while it was still moist, show a distinct similarity in artistic style. Many of the sarcophagi were faced with marble, and were engraved with names, memorials, and chiselled figures in relief. Such work would have been carried out by jobbing craftsmen, and so it is not surprising to see classical Roman motifs, such as the peacock, images of viticulture, and the beardless philosopher figure dressed in tunic and sandals. Yet these are images transformed by ritual and symbol so that they take on a whole new meaning rich in biblical allusions. So, for example, the common carved image of a bunch of harvested grapes would recall for the Christian how they themselves were grafted into Christ, the true vine, and trigger a range of associations connected to the Eucharist and its sacrificial cup. In other words, the whole ensemble of images and emblems was reconfigured and functioned in an *anamnetic* way, that is, in a quasi-sacramental way in making visible the invisible presence of Christ, and in mediating the truths of God's saving work. Yet the images chosen are not pictures in the sense that we would understand the term, illustrating a narrative, with background and attendant figures depicting a story, but rather single and seemingly unconnected figures in an almost cartoon style. And while they could be read symbolically by Christians they could also have another quite different and harmless significance to the pagans who came upon them. This is true not only of the wheat and grapes but also of the shepherd figure and of the depiction of groups of figures at table, frequently used in the art of the catacombs.

The purpose of art in the catacombs then, was not to illustrate a story, but to convey through images the Christian faith, professed at baptism, 'in the resurrection of the body and the life everlasting'. Christians of the third century occupied a social and religious world that was more sensitive and responsive to symbolic meaning than our own. Theirs was a sacramental and not a scientific view of the world, and when they entered a building for worship, they had a sense of entering a sacramental world, which engaged all the senses.

This concept of the sacramental function of Christian art continued after the end of persecution into the age of the building of the great basilicas. At Ravenna the mosaics, as in many other areas of Byzantine influence, were intended to be much more than decorative illustration. They filled baptisteries and churches with a symphony of colour and dancing light. Colour, composition and forms, depicted in small glass cubes or *tesserae*, unevenly set so as to catch and refract, at different angles, the flickering light which would strike them, gave the illusion of being alive. The effect, of course, was deliberate and intensified the revelatory experience of the art as complementing the witness of the Word, manifesting the form of the saving and sanctifying presence of God in Christ and in the lives of the saints. To Orthodox theologians such as John Damascene Christian iconography was a very medium for the Christian's participation in the divine life shown in the figure (of Christ, Mary the God-bearer, or one of the saints) or saving event depicted. The icon, as we have seen, made manifest to the one who prayed before it the concealed divine reality, which might otherwise be hidden, unnoticed, or simply overlooked, for 'Every image is declarative and indicative of something hidden . . . the image is given for the sake of guiding knowledge and manifesting publicly that which is concealed.' Yet not everyone saw things this way. As we have already seen there were also within the eastern tradition those who abhorred the use of icons as in some way demeaning the Godhead by humanizing it. Though the Orthodox tradition of iconography was finally vindicated in 843 CE much art had been destroyed during the reign of the Iconoclasts. However, one beneficial effect was to have caused the theology of icon painting to be refined under persecution. A tradition of Christian image-making was later to flourish again among the Slavs by whom it was taken to the land of the Russ where it finally reached its zenith in the fifteenth-century devotional art of Holy Russia.

In the West, Christian art flourished from the time of the baptism of Clovis (500 CE). The motivation for the making of Christian artefacts and the decoration of churches, manuscripts and service books was here that of 'giving of glory to God'. This artistic impulse reached its full flowering during the time of Charlemagne's Holy Roman Empire, when the ancient sculptural art of imperial Rome was seen as the apogee of artistic perfection and again in the glorious Romanesque and Gothic churches of the twelfth-century Renaissance. Henceforward the western tradition based on the model of a Christian empire flourished independently of the eastern tradition guided by aesthetic and monastic traditions. Yet lines of artistic influence did, inevitably, cross political boundaries. Celtic art as exemplified in the Lindisfarne Gospels, a port-folio of interlacing geometric patterns, exquisitely painted figures and animal forms, had its roots in the Coptic monastic art of Egypt, and found its way to what is now northern Italy by missionary monks such as Columbanus (543–615). In 567 the reluctant missionary Augustine is said to have brought an icon of Christ from Rome to England and thereby introduced iconic art to the Anglo-Saxon Church. The early eighth-century English church historian, Bede, also tells how the seventh-century Northumbrian monk Benedict Biscop brought icons from his travels to Rome and how he decorated his church at Wearmouth with the figures of Mary and the saints over the central arch, a series of Gospel scenes running along the south wall, and illustrations of the Revelation of St John along the north wall (Brown and Loades, 1995, p. 126). It is hardly surprising therefore that many of the people inhabit-ing illuminated manuscripts from Anglo-Saxon England are based on figures as drawn by icon painters in the East with their flowing stylized draperies and huge, lozenge-shaped eyes.

From the seventh to the eleventh centuries, not only manuscript illu-mination but other aspects of artistic style, media and craft, such as enamelling, metal work, mosaic, fresco and tapestry, were borrowed and copied by those who had travelled through the East on pilgrimage to Constantinople and Jerusalem. As towns and cities grew along the trade routes, from east to west from Jerusalem to recaptured Moorish Spain, and from north to south, from Jarrow to Rome, they became productive intersections of medieval art and culture (Duby, 2000). Yet the artistry, craftsmanship, and sheer visual extravagance which went into the decoration of churches and monasteries were also underpinned by a theological aesthetic to do all for the glory of God. The statuary, wall paintings, glass and ornaments with their rich medley of forms, figures and colours were designed to trigger the memory of Christian meaning and to enrich the store of Christian imagination. Hence to enter a church like the Abbey of St Denis was to step into a virtual mirror of the celestial city with its heavenly hosts set in the terrestrial urban context, and there to catch something of the transfiguring splendour of God's beauty. It was intended to be the architectural and artistic translation of the vision of the holy city described by St John the Divine, 'having the glory of God, its radiance like a most rare jewel . . . clear as crystal' (Revelation 21.10ff.). The vision in Revelation also tells how 'the kings of the earth bring into it the glory of the honour of the nations'. Churches like St Denis depended upon and drew the gifts and resources of the nobility and royal patronage. Yet, not surprisingly, their brilliance also drew critical attention.

The mid-twelfth century saw the breaking down of the hegemony of the Benedictines in Europe, with the establishing of cathedrals, staffed by secular Canons Regular. Here, one might think of Chartres Cathedral with its array of sculpture and sumptuous stained glass, depicting the established repertoire of biblical typology, giving form to scriptural figures and radiating the presence of the same mysterious God found at St Denis, through a diffused and multicoloured light. Such windows running at a high level were not intended to give a view of the outside, but to capture the light, and filter it in such a way as to illuminate the building in shifting shafts of light with the passing time of day. Reflection on the play of light gave rise to the thought that the kind of light required in a place of worship was not strictly utilitarian, enabling worshippers to see, but was designed that they might be illuminated by the light of God revealed in Christ and reflected in the saints. In the scholastic period a formal distinction between 'light' and 'illumination' also played a key part in the development of scholastic aesthetic theory.

St Bernard of Clairvaux recognized the value of art in churches to inspire and to impress the Christian story upon ordinary worshippers. Yet he questioned the use of such art, too, especially in the monasteries. He lamented not only the expense, but also the absurdity of some of the decoration in cloisters, chapter houses and churches. Hence the Cistercians repudiated all figural art in their churches, and built their abbeys on the frontiers of society, in a deliberate withdrawal from the world into a life of simple interiority. The primary task of the monk was to the Cistercians to focus the inner eye, and to construct an inner imaginative framework in which to contemplate the things and ways of God (Carruthers, 1998). Yet the simplicity of their churches was not without its own aesthetic. The architectural language itself was eloquent, and the use of grisaille glass both in the church and the chapter house was a means of filtering a pure quality of light in their search not simply for 'light', but also for illumination and inner enlightenment. So, although early Cistercian churches are devoid of all figural art, carving and statuary (apart from a statue of their patron, the Blessed Virgin Mary), they are cavernous architectural spaces, monumental statements to remind us that space as well as shelter is required by those who gather for worship.

The architectural style of Gothic architecture with its soaring arches, lofty pinnacles, pointed windows and voluminous spaces, continued the search for transcendence in an architectural form. Developments in the technology of building led to the refining of ribbed vaulting and to the narrowing of roof piers and columns in the nave that had hitherto borne the downward weight of the roof. Supported by externally arched buttressing, the walls could now be both thinner and taller than their Romanesque predecessors and a repeated series of open arches gave the viewer at ground level a sense of the building's verticality. Windows could also be much larger than in Romanesque churches thus encouraging the flowering of the art of stained glass. On entering a Gothic building one's eyes are lifted, one's sights raised by the deliberate architectural lines, in order that one might look above and beyond the mundane level and field of vision and human commerce. The very building itself is again inspired by the vision of the new Jerusalem, and the worship in these buildings, most famously perhaps in Salisbury in worship according to the Sarum Rite, was full of processions so that the worshippers felt as if they were walking the streets of the celestial Salem, the very city in which the Paschal Lamb, who was slain, was at its very heart and the centre of their praises. Throughout the Middle Ages to the eve of the Reformation cathedrals, churches and oratories continued to be galleries of figures carved in wood and stone, images and colour. Yet radical voices were soon to question this and to unleash an aniconic reaction both in England and on the continent.

Some of this was fuelled by preachers such as Savonarola in Italy, John Hus in Bohemia and by John Wyclif in England. There was also an implied criticism of the opulence of the Church in the face of crying social need and poverty. Yet other factors also played their part such as greed and a latent iconoclasm. Those who benefited from the dissolution of the monasteries in England, for example, were not the poor but the aristocracy and the rising gentry and Thomas Cromwell could always find those who were willing to carry out acts of vandalism in the name of the law. In this milieu, however, the Church of England attempted to steer a middle way. The Ten Articles of 1536 allowed images in churches reckoning them to be 'representers of virtue and good example . . . the kindlers and firers of men's minds'. Yet preachers were also enjoined to warn the 'rude people' against acts of superstition and the dangers of idolatry. The *via media* continued for the most part during the reigns of Henry VIII and Elizabeth I and was later enshrined in the writings of such men as Richard Hooker and George Herbert (see Chapter 1). Yet there were also outbreaks of iconoclasm, usually as a means of political expediency between 1536 and 1540 at the dissolution of the monasteries, in 1550 during the minority of Edward VI and again under the Articles of Enquiry of 1559. As part of this latter 'enquiry', intended to placate the more Puritan wing of the Church of England (which had fled to Geneva during the reign of Mary and was only now returning home under Elizabeth I), the royal commissioners were empowered to oversee the destruction of all images which 'were the cause of idolatry'. The rood lofts and figures of Mary and John either side of the crucifix, restored under Mary, fuelled bonfires that also destroyed works of art and other devotional objects. (Two years later, in many parish churches the supporting beam of the rood was to become the base for a board painted with the crest of the royal arms!) However, the injunctions required also that the church fabric had to be repaired and put in good order if damaged by the removal of proscribed images, and furnishings. Not so in the time of the Civil War and during the Cromwellian Protectorate when iconoclasm again flourished, often carried out by the soldiery not only out of religious motives but also so that they might supplement their meagre pay.

A great deal of anti-Roman propaganda was directed in Elizabethan times and again in the early seventeenth century against what was seen as the extravagant decoration and ornamentation of Roman churches. Yet there were also contrary voices. William Laud (1573–1645), who had to guard himself against accusations of popery, lamented the loss of the beauty of holiness and expressed the opinion that there was 'little necessity, God knows, to preach or print against too much adorning of churches among us, where yet so many churches lie very nastily in many places of the kingdom, and no one too much adorned to be found' (Milton, 1995, p. 315). The 1630s saw Laud rise to a position of power and influence and to his appointment by Charles I as Archbishop of Canterbury in 1633. His efforts to enhance the setting of the liturgy are well known, although it is probably true to say that he was more of an aggressive propagandist than a popular innovator (Maltby, 1998, pp. 108, 122). Laud regarded the altar as the proper visual focus of a church, and promoted the return of the altar to its former position against the wall of the east end, the placing of candlesticks on the altar and setting up of altar rails to demark a sacred space. At Laud's direction the windows of the chapel at Lambeth Palace and in Canterbury cathedral were reglazed with stained glass imagery, actions which led to the accusation being made at his trial in 1644 that he had reintroduced popish superstition.

In the seventeenth century parish church worship was conducted 'decently and in order' according to the rubrics of the Prayer Book. Yet the polychromatic interior of the church and statuary of the medieval church had long since gone. Art work, as permitted by one of the Canons of 1604, was a worked and lettered wooden board, often framed by carved wooden pilasters, on which was displayed the texts of the Creed, Decalogue (Ten Commandments) and the Lord's Prayer. These panels, many of which survived well into the nineteenth century, and a few of which can be seen even today, provided an artistic focal point, and were a clear statement of the shift in visual attention from figurative art to typography. A common concession to religious figurative art were the Old Testament figures of Moses, often shown dressed in the garb of a prophet, and Aaron, dressed in the vestments of the high priest. Tapestries depicting these and other Old Testament figures were not an unknown form of decoration, especially in collegiate or private chapels. John Cosin, while Bishop of Durham, had a tapestry depicting the visit of the Queen of Sheba to King Solomon (which in medieval Christian iconography was taken as a type of the Epiphany visitation of the Magi to the infant Christ) hung as a reredos behind the altar in the chapel at Auckland Castle. A landmark legal case concerning the introduction of pictorial art of New Testament subjects was heard in 1684, in the Court of Arches. The incumbent and parishioners of Maulton, in Lincolnshire, had petitioned for a faculty to hang pictures of the apostles on the east wall of the parish church. The application, having been refused by both the bishop and the diocesan chancellor, was approved by the appeal court on condition that the pictures were not used for superstitious or idolatrous purposes (Addleshaw and Etchells, 1948, p. 161). Attention was also given in this period to funerary art. In the recumbent figures of Tudor and Stuart gentlemen and their wives there is a studied piety but a hint also that it was now perhaps the deeds of man which were of importance rather than the deeds of God. This is particularly apparent in the funerary monuments at Tong in Shropshire, most of which date from this period and which completely obscure the view of the communion table in the chancel.

Recent studies have shown that in the eighteenth century the Church was far from being somnolent. A great number of churches were refurbished, and a number of new churches were built, such as Nicholas Hawksmoor's famous London churches. These new churches, far from being merely elegant auditoria for preaching, were designed to facilitate worship modelled on the pattern of primitive Christians in their Roman imperial basilicas (Doll, 1997). This eighteenth-century classical model of design gave equal weight and dignity to the preaching of the word and to the celebration of the sacraments and what now looks to be a static and fixed arrangement was in fact far from the case. Box pews in the nave certainly became fashionable, and there the people sat below the clerk and the priest for the ministry of the word. Yet when the Eucharist was celebrated, the congregation would move from their places to gather around the altar for the celebration of the mystery of mysteries, the commemoration of Christ's death and the looking forward to his coming in glory, thus giving real meaning to those immortal words of the Book of Common Prayer 'Draw near with faith . . .'.

In these churches the sanctuaries, and sometimes chancels, were paved with black and white marble, arranged in geometric patterns. The chancel ceiling was invariably painted, and the semi-domed ceiling over the altar adorned with stucco foliage patterned decoration. The altar, though often relatively small in its dimensions, was seemly, and generally dressed with fine fabric, silk, or a folding velvet covering with matching tasselled cushions on which to rest the service book. In some cases, the altar was given added dignity by being covered by a two- or four-columned decorated baldachin. In most churches the Decalogue board was now fixed to the east wall, forming a kind of reredos, but in some of the wealthier churches, painted altarpieces, some in rather ostentatious baroque style, were commissioned and fixed to the east wall. The Grinling Gibbons altarpiece above the altar in Wren's church of St James, Piccadilly (built in 1684), was of a pelican, plucking her breast to feed her young, a symbolic emblem of Christ feeding his people in the Eucharist (Addleshaw and Etchells, 1948, pp. 159–60).

Another, and more frequent, artistic form of decoration relating to an understanding of the Eucharist was the dove, representing the Holy Spirit, through whom the fruits of the Eucharist are realized. Unlike the Eucharistic Prayers in the ASB and *Common Worship* which accord a significant part to the Holy Spirit in the celebration of the Eucharist, in the so-called *epiclesis*, any reference, let alone an invocation of the Holy Spirit, is conspicuously absent in the Consecration Prayer of the 1662 Communion Service. So what we have in this instance is the use of art to compensate for what was regarded as being a deficient liturgical form. Again, given the singular emphasis on Christ's death and passion in the text of the 1662 communion rite, a number of these painted altarpieces significantly portrayed an aspect of the Easter mystery. St Mary,

Coslany, Norwich, had a painting of the risen Christ, and at considerable expense, the parish of St Mary Redcliffe, Bristol, commissioned a Hogarth painting of the ascension. Such figurative art, though exceptional in ordinary parish churches, marked the return of the placing of paintings within a sacred setting. These were intended not only to beautify the house of God, but again, as in the early church buildings we have studied, to extend the meaning of what happened liturgically in that setting.

In the nineteenth century such developments in liturgical arrangements and decoration gave way to an increasing sense of an ordered beauty of holiness in the churches of the so-called Oxford Movement. The impetus for this movement came from the Tractarians, a group of Oxford scholars led by Keble, Newman, Froude and Pusey. Their success lay in seizing the political moment by asserting the independence of the Church as a distinctive divine society, called to live out its holiness in continuity with the tradition of the apostles. More generally, their influence lay in raising the sacramental consciousness of the Church, and in showing the central place of the Eucharist in the Church's self-understanding and worship. Thus they spawned the Catholic movement which sought to restore to the Church the furnishings, devotional practices, and liturgical ceremonies which had been repudiated and discarded at the Reformation. The movement, however was far from homogenous, and interesting parallels and influences can be identified from other cultural movements and artistic tendencies. There was, for instance, a romanticism and fascination with things medieval and Gothic in artistic and cultural circles, while the pre-Raphaelite painters, Rossetti, Millais and Hunt, sought to recover a symbolic language in their paintings of religious subjects in a naturalistic setting. Their work was championed by the social critic and art historian, John Ruskin, who in *The Stones of Venice* celebrated the achievements of the early Gothic style.

The Tractarians sought to identify the locus of authority in the Church, and to forge a more adequate ecclesiology for the Church of England, but the Anglo-Catholic ecclesiologists of the same period had a rather narrower focus and goal. What concerned them was the setting and accoutrements of Catholic worship. In 1839 the hymnologist J. M. Neale and Benjamin Webb founded the Cambridge Camden Society (from 1846 known as the Ecclesiological Society) with the expressed aim 'to promote the study of Ecclesiastical Architecture and Antiquities, and the restoration of mutilated architectural remains'.

A number of new churches were built according to these principles. One famous example is Pusey's church of St Saviour in an impoverished area of the industrial city of Leeds. Here, as in the Catholic churches in London's East End, the style of worship and the elaborate ceremonial brought an element of theatre, colour and mystery to compensate for the drab and dull surroundings in which the church was set and in which its worshippers lived. The architectural setting for catholic ceremonial worship was taken to be fourteenth century decorated pointed Gothic. Thus they looked to the past, and in their rebuilding and reordering of churches had a wanton disregard of the immediate past and its ecclesiastical furnishings and fittings. The pious architect Augustus Welby Pugin (1812–52) argued with a simple logic that as Gothic architecture had emerged from within an all-pervasive Catholic culture, then it represented the apogee of Christian architectural style. Butterfield's Church of All Saints, Margaret Street, with its dark interior decorated with mosaics, glazed tiling, metalwork, painted devotional statue of the Blessed Virgin Mary, rood figures, and reredos behind the altar, was taken as a model studio of Anglo-Catholic worship. More recent studies have drawn attention to the fact that such decorative schemes concealed an arbitrary historical judgement regarding a supposed 'golden age', and stood more as a symbol of Catholic allegiance rather than of a new Christian aesthetic (Reed, 1998).

The legacy of the nineteenth-century Catholic revival for the early twentieth century was a renewed appreciation of the importance of the church building. The church came to be generally regarded as being more than a setting for worship. It was a sacramental sign of the presence of God in the world. Such a view persisted and was articulated in the 1930s by the celebrated Anglo-Catholic artist and architect, Ninian Comper, when he wrote that:

> A church built with hands . . . is the outward expression here on earth of that spiritual Church built of living stones, the Bride of Christ, *Urbs beata Jerusalem*, which stretches back to the foundation of the world and onwards to all eternity. (Comper, 1936)

Among Anglicans George Bell, Bishop of Chichester from 1929 to 1958, was also exceptional in his concern for artists and the place of art in the Church. His enthronement sermon at Chichester was a rallying call for a real dialogue and the harnessing of the arts to the worship of the Church (Jasper, 1967, chapter 7). Bell befriended the German artist Hans Feibusch, who had fled from Nazi Germany, and was instrumental in bringing Walter Hussey to Chichester to be dean of the cathedral. As vicar of St Matthew's, Northampton, Hussey had shown a passion for modern art and although he was a rather aloof character, proved himself to be an adept networker. He persuaded the sculptor Henry Moore to carve a Madonna and Child for St Matthew's and at the service of dedication for the work persuaded Graham Sutherland to paint a crucifixion for the church. At Chichester Hussey was to seek another commission from Sutherland, a *Noli me Tangere*, which captures the emotionally charged moment of encounter between Mary Magdalen and the risen Christ. John Piper was commissioned to design an altar frontal, Cecil Collins an icon of the *Divine Light*, and finally Marc Chagall to make his richly coloured and evocative medley of praise in stained glass, *Arts to the Glory of God*, illustrating Psalm 150. Hussey's achievement was inspiring, but alas he was an exception. As Keith Walker has shown in his book *Images and Idols?* the relationship between the Church and the arts in the twentieth century has often been rather hesitant as where two worlds have failed largely to meet and to meaningfully interact. This has not only been true within Anglicanism but also in the Roman Catholic Church. As the story of the liturgical arts movement in America (which we will look at in more detail later) shows there was a profound lack of dialogue between the Catholic Church and the world of art until the time of the Second Vatican Council, and even today there is a tendency for the Church to see itself as the arbiter of aesthetic taste which must educate the artist rather than being willing to enter into a real debate about art and theology and the relationship between them (Constitution on the Mass, 2000). This is nowhere more clear than in the criticism which was levelled by the Vatican at those who had the vision to commission a variety of artists, both Christian and non-Christian, to work on the church at Assy in France in the 1940s and 1950s (See Apostolos-Cappadona, *Art, Creativity, and the Sacred*; see also Chapter 3 below).

For the question is not simply one of commissioning and placing art in churches, but relates to the whole dialogue between art and theology, which Bell, for one, considered to be of vital importance for the worship and ministry of the Church. A recent incident reported in the press concerning the withdrawal of a commission to design and execute a new font for St Paul's Cathedral, London underlines the issue. The artist in question is the 1991 Turner prize-winner, Anish Kapoor, who at the invitation of Friedhelm Mennekes exhibited his work at St Peter's Church, Cologne. For St Paul's Cathedral, Kapoor had proposed a vast circular black granite font which, appropriately for the celebration of the sacrament of baptism, would hold a considerable volume of water. Above the font, Kapoor proposed large mirror domes to be suspended from the ceiling. The projected piece would have been entirely congruous placed on the spacious black and white marble floor in the seventeenth-century interior of the cathedral.

Whatever the circumstances of the withdrawal of a commission, one must ask whether this is yet another instance of the Church's failure to engage with artists. If so then the challenge for the churches as they enter the twenty-first century must be to seek ways of finding a new discourse to speak of the things of God in a postmodern world. For in such a visual world as the one we inhabit it is imperative for the Church to enter into dialogue with artists. Only then might we come to a deeper appreciation of what it is to be open to the transcendent, and to glimpse something of the divine in what is increasingly perceived to be a God-forsaken and brutally ugly world.

Chapter 3

Encounter and Communication in Placing Art in Churches

The experience of Anish Kapoor and the cancellation of the commission for St Paul's is in many ways symptomatic of a difficult relationship between the worlds of church and art which goes back several centuries. As Jane Dillenberger comments:

> From the death of Rembrandt in 1669 . . . there was a hiatus in the creation of religious art. Some few artists created paintings with religious subject matter, and some works of art were commissioned by the church. But the volume and quantity of these individual works and commissions ebbed. (Jane Dillenberger, 1986, p. 200)

In the Protestant churches the claims of the written word became pre-eminent, not only in the writings of theologians such as Barth and Bultmann but also in the building of new churches where the pulpit, with its emphasis on the preaching of the word, was the focal point. In the Roman Catholic Church such art as was commissioned tended to be conservative both in its iconography and style treating the artist still as fabricator rather than creator. Artists, for their part, began to look for self-expression and self-fulfilment and as such many came to have qualms about producing works of art which at times have been 'inappropriate if not inimical to ancient sacred themes'. But why did this happen? How deep-rooted is the communication problem between the Church and artists? And what can we do to repair this relationship as we emerge into a new century and indeed into a new millennium?

The first reason why communication has broken down between the Church and many artists has to do, seemingly, with a certain arrogance on the part of the Church which at times has seen itself as the moral arbiter par excellence, responsible not only for decisions about what art is suitable for use in church (in terms of iconography and style), but also for decisions about what artists should be commissioned in the first place. In the minds of some this has meant that Christian art, and particularly art which is to be placed in Christian churches, is only acceptable if it is the work of a Christian artist. One is reminded here of the attitude of the Pharisees who were concerned only with *by what authority* Jesus acted (Mark 11.27–28) rather than with the quality of his teaching and ministry. There is also a parallel with those who, like John Wyclif in England and John Hus in Bohemia at the turn of the fourteenth and fifteenth centuries, claimed that the efficacy of the sacraments depended on the worthiness of the one who administers them.

Against those who like Jacques Maritain in the debate over Assy tried to confine 'Christian art' to Christian artists (John Dillenberger, 1996, p. 199) it is possible to argue that Christ did not sit only with the Pharisees and the other worthies of Jewish society but also with Roman centurions, tax collectors and sinners that all might taste of the heavenly banquet (Luke 14.1–24). Moreover if we accept that creation is part of God's work as the master artist, and that we are created in God's image and are co-creators with him, then it follows that by our very humanity we are all called, whatever our background, to be part of the artistic process, making or arranging what we conceive to be truth in some symbolic manner whether or not we do so consciously for the glory of God (Spencer, 1998, p. 26). If this is the case, should the Church examine the faith or the moral background of those who work for it as artists? Yet such discrimination has been a worrying theme throughout the whole history of the relationship between the Church and the artist and not only in the distant past. The great sculptor Sir Jacob Epstein was a victim of this when he offered his totemic 'Behold the Man' as a gift to Selby Abbey in Yorkshire. Although the rector was pleased with the gift the Parochial Church Council (PCC) refused to countenance it and the sculpture was never installed (Walker, 1996, p. 3). One wonders if this was because the artist was Jewish or because another work of Epstein had been condemned in the 1920s as 'pornographic'. At Assy, the fact that non-Catholic and indeed non-Christian artists were employed in the decorative scheme for the church and were allowed complete freedom in the execution of their work, led to hostility and suspicion by the Vatican for the work which was only brought to fruition by the determination and vision of Canon Jean Devémy and Fr M.-A. Couturier who believed that for the most part pious artists produced banal work (John Dillenberger, 1996, p. 199).

Debates on the worthiness of the artist have also coincided with the tendency within the Church to take an entrenched and rather traditionalist attitude towards what is suitable art for introducing into a Christian place of worship. This was the situation faced in the twentieth century by the Liturgical Arts Movement in the USA. Established in 1928 and led by lay and religious from all levels of the Roman Catholic Church, the movement aimed to devise ways and means of improving standards, taste, craftsmanship and liturgical correctness in the practice of Roman Catholic art (White, 1990, p. viii). Yet it encountered many problems. The first was that many of the leading Roman Catholic artists were earning their bread and butter on churches in the neo-Gothic style, introduced into America by James Renwick, and could not really afford to be creative rather than imitative as the movement's most influential leader Maurice Lavanoux demanded (White, 1990, p. 148). The second problem was that although Lavanoux himself was able in the end to have an influence on the Sacred Commission for Art in the Liturgy in the 1950s and 1960s, for much of its history the Liturgical Arts Movement was running contrary to the papacy in its ethos and beliefs. The movement claimed that modern art was eminently suitable for church use because the abstract quality of modern art corresponded to the abstract quality of mystical experiences and because modern art as an expression of time and place is a function of life in community (White, 1990, p. 156). At the same time, however, Pope Pius XI (on the occasion of the opening of the Vatican picture gallery in 1932) was condemning that same art as 'unfitting for service in the church because it reverts to the crude forms of the darkest ages'. He therefore advised that contemporary art 'should be excluded from the building, remodelling and decoration of churches' (*Mediator Dei*, 1947) and denounced those forms of art which shocked Christian taste, modesty and devotion.

In recent years the official attitude of the Roman Catholic Church towards modern art and its use in churches has changed. Paul VI in his encyclical *Le nobili espressioni* apologized to artists for the way in which the Church had imposed imitation and style on them down the centuries against creativity. At the same time the *Constitution on the Sacred Liturgy*, in its chapter on sacred art and furnishings, affirms the development of new relationships between the Church and artists and encourages bishops and others in authority to seek out the best in the religious art of our own day. Yet the *Constitution* also talks about the responsibility of bishops to educate artists into suitable iconographical schemes, and this is where part of the danger lies. For what is a suitable iconographical scheme? And who is to decide its suitability?

At Assy Canon Devémy and Fr Couturier worked closely with each artist on exploring individual themes from Christian iconography which best suited the character of each. This resulted in a scheme where the saints and evangelists were well-represented, but in which only one sacrament, baptism, featured in the work of Marc Chagall. Devémy and Couturier believed strongly that the artist must be given freedom in which to operate if both the best artists of the day were to accept commissions there and if their work was to be inspiring rather than banal. Their work, however, has been criticized on the grounds that a church without an iconographic scheme lacks religious ambience and feels more like a museum (cf. John Dillenberger, 1996, p. 198). Meanwhile the Vatican, too, refused to have anything to do with Assy on the grounds that modern art and unbelief went hand in hand.

In England more recently there has been fierce debate over two other works of art, *Sound II* in Winchester Cathedral and *The Messenger,* a temporary video image installed at Durham Cathedral by the American artist Bill Viola as part of the UK Year of the Visual Arts in 1996. *Sound II* was given by the artist Antony Gormley to Winchester Cathedral in 1994 on the condition that the dean and chapter prepare the crypt, the artist's chosen setting for the figure, to receive it. The fact that the crypt is partially under water for three months of the year enhances the figure whose own hands are raised in a gesture of cupping water to the face. Symbolically there can be no doubt of the connection here between water and life. To the Christian viewer there is also a connection with the theme of baptism and the rising from the dark waters of death to new life. The dean and chapter were happy to receive the gift and installed it in the crypt where it has been an object of contemplation to many: visitors, pilgrims and congregation members alike. Yet its place in the life of the community has not always been so assured. As in the case of all Gormley's sculptures *Sound II* is based on the figure of an unclothed male (the artist uses himself as a model for all his castings.). There is nothing erotic about it, rather it is a thing of simplicity and beauty. Yet at the time of its installation there was some disquiet about the placing of a naked figure, however innocent, in a church setting.

Viola's installation at Durham focused unapologetically, among other things, on the full-length figure of a naked man. This caused the dean at the time of the installation to consult with the police. Yet pornography played no part here, any more than it did at Winchester with *Sound II.* The figure of the man was at first hardly identifiable amid the deep dark waters which surrounded him. As he revolved in the water he slowly rose up and finally broke the surface as he took in an enormous and audible gulp of air. To the pilgrim the image represented God emerging from the void to utter first cries of creation, the birth of Adam or Christ emerging from the tomb. Also, although the figure was naked, the colours which washed over one side of the body were suggestive of draperies should the viewer feel that the figure needed them. Yet cries of consternation because of the man's nakedness led to the image being screened off from the gaze of children and those who might be offended and those who wished to see it were made to think themselves as voyeurs rather than as worshippers or pilgrims.

The particular conservatism which attitudes to *Sound II* and *The Messenger* display in many ways echoes a more general conservatism of which David Stancliffe writes concerning the large number of churchgoers who are unaware of any sense of development in architecture and in the liturgical setting of worship. They imagine, he comments, that the Church as they know it is how it has always been. Many churches, he believes, are frozen in a period which reflects a particular social order and a didactic style of worship in which the congregation rarely expect to meet God (Stancliffe, 1995, pp. 44–58). And if many Christians are immured from encountering God in the church buildings with which they are familiar, then they are perhaps even less likely to imagine that they could ever encounter God in more controversial and contemporary works of art such as *Sound II* and *The Messenger*. The reception of the work of another contemporary artist, Roger Wagner, underlines this conservatism still further. Wagner's paintings of the *Easter Breakfast*, of the *Life of Simon Stylites* and of *Ruth and Boaz* are far less controversial than either *Sound II* or *The Messenger*. Using traditional iconography and representational painting they have an appeal which would fit into even a traditional setting. Yet his work also has a modern twist. Alongside the figures of Ruth and Boaz and some sheep there are also empty oil drums and a discarded tractor wheel to remind us that the lives of modern nomads are far from idyllic and far from precious. Yet perhaps it is this very lack of preciousness in the work of Wagner that has meant that hitherto his work has not been patronized by the Church. At the same time his work is too religious and figurative to appeal to many contemporary galleries and has so far only found a place in the Ashmolean Museum in Oxford and in the Fitzwilliam Museum in Cambridge (Cranfield, 2001).

Finally, there has also been a tendency within the churches to view art as an evangelistic tool rather than allowing it to have an intrinsic value and purpose in itself. This has led to yet further conservatism about what is acceptable art for use within churches. In order to avoid the controversy which such works as *Sound II* and *The Messenger* originally engendered many churches have tended to look instead to art which is 'safe' not only in its use of traditional iconography but in its romanticism also. Yet such art has not always been the best available and at times has been frankly second rate.

Such an attitude, where it is prevalent, has hardly endeared the Church to the world of art. Bruce Whitney Hermann, himself now a well-known Christian artist in the United States, writes powerfully about how, when he was growing up in Protestant America in the 1960s, he had felt let down by the pictures of Christ which he encountered, which unlike the music and the stained glass he came across he found sentimental and postcard pretty (Hermann, 1998, p. 85). This sense of disappointment led Hermann to turn his back on Christianity and to seek a home in eastern philosophy before returning to Christianity in the early 1980s. Since then he has painted prolifically on Old and New Testament themes. Perhaps his most powerful work is his paintings on the trial and crucifixion of Christ which he has gathered together in a book entitled *Golgotha: The Passion in Word and Image*. These paintings are full of recognizable Christian iconography on the suffering servant but the power of expression and technique used by the artist ensures that they can never be accused of the sentimentalism which Hermann himself found so abhorrent in his own early encounters with Christian art.

Using art for evangelistic purposes is also inimical to the way that art is viewed by most artists. For them art can have no objective purpose but must be allowed to be art for its own sake. This springs from a Kantian view of things which believes (after Plato) in the existence of an aesthetic subjective reality which has an existence apart from objectivity. According to this way of looking at things art is answerable only to itself. Not only should art not be evaluated by objective criteria, and allowed to be for art's sake, but it also has no social or religious responsibility outside itself. Thus the use of art for any objective end, including evangelism, is an abuse of art itself. And so where the Church has tended to insist that art, where used in churches, must have an evangelistic message, artists have chosen to avoid ecclesiastical commissions and to place their art, even where it has a religious theme or iconography, in secular galleries or in sculpture parks since here they are generally allowed to speak in their own way to those who encounter them. A work such as William Pye's *Water Cube* (2000) in the sculpture park at Roche Court may speak to the Christian of a baptismal font and of the waters of life. But no such direct symbolism is intended and the onlooker may read into the work what he or she wills. Yet when an artist is commissioned to design a font for a Christian church (as in the current discussions between Pye and the dean and chapter of Salisbury Cathedral) his work must be prepared to accept the whole weight which history and traditional iconography places upon it. While a few artists, such as Pye himself and also from the recent past John Piper, Marc Chagall, Georges Rouault and Graham Sutherland, are prepared to rise to this challenge, many other artists are not.

There have also been difficulties for many artists in the way that the Church commissions works of art. When looking at a design for approval the Cathedrals Fabric Commission and most Diocesan Advisory Committees normally require the artist at an early stage in the design process (and well before approval is given for the project) to produce detailed drawings and specifications concerning the work of art and the colours and materials in which it is to be executed, as well as details of its size and where it is to be placed. While some details (such as the placing of a work of art and materials to be used) are important for early consideration, the expectation, often present in the mind of approving committees, that the finished piece will look exactly as it did at the design stage is erroneous and is likely to cause difficulties in ongoing communication with the artist. For what those commissioning the work or approving it must understand is that if it is a living thing no work of art will look exactly as it did on the design. In the case of a stained glass window, for example, the difference between light flooding through a window and a painted design on paper can often be quite dramatic. And though a sculptor can, and often does, have a certain form in mind when the design is conceived, the final shape and form of the sculpture will normally depend on the medium used, especially if that medium has its own intrinsic form like wood or stone. Once the artist begins a work, if it is to live, it will need to be allowed to develop and may well take on subtle changes not in the original plans. This is a matter of trust to be developed between the artist and those commissioning the work who, if they are to grant integrity to the artist as a creator rather than as a mere fabricator, can and must leave a number of creative decisions to the artist along the way. That way a creative partnership will be formed and the resulting work of art will become a thing of life and beauty which transcends the expectations of all those who have been involved in its creation from conception to completion.

Such a sensitive working together will almost always improve the relationship between individual artists and those wishing to commission their work. Yet there are still problems of language which need to be overcome. Churches, as patrons of the arts, tend to think in terms of theology and iconography. Artists on the other hand think more usually in terms of image or form, light and shade. Many artists tend to work in non-discursive forms that proceed from intuition rather than well-rehearsed facts, while churches tend to come together because they agree on truths (such as a creed, or sacred book) and, although they rely on symbols, their meaning and use is invariably regulated by doctrinal understandings (Walton, 1998, pp. 112–13). Moreover, whereas within the history of the churches there has been a tendency at times towards employing all in the service of evangelism, there has been a tendency within modern art and post-modern art to be bitterly iconoclastic. A good example of this is the provocatively titled *Last Supper* by Damien Hirst, recently acquired by the Tate Gallery. This group consisted of six pieces depicting typed labels of food which might or might not be polluted and cause death by poisoning. Another example was the Royal Academy's recent exhibition *Apocalypse 2000*. Situated as it was in a secular gallery and freed from the specific religious framework of the past or of a church commission, *Apocalypse 2000* replaced the terrifying vision of the Last Things in the book of Revelation with a more general celebration of beauty and horror. In this case, however, the dissociation of the word 'apocalypse' from its traditional

Jewish and Christian roots did not really free the artists to rise to new heights but led instead to an exhibition in which everything seemed somehow to have lost its power and sense of urgency.

So what can we do about this problem of communication between the Church and the artistic world? The key would seem to lie in education – both in art colleges and in the Church. Within art colleges art history has traditionally been divided into different artistic periods of time such as the Pre-Raphaelites or Modernism. What has been studied here is the leading artists of the day and their achievements in terms of materials or technique. Yet an equally valid way of looking at art history would be to look at the treatment of certain themes across the centuries. In this way the nativity could be included in the theme of depictions of birth within art and the crucifixion within depictions of death in art. Evidence suggests that where such a thematic approach has been taken it has engendered a great deal of interest as in the *Seeing Salvation* exhibition in the National Gallery and in its accompanying television series.

Equally, more needs to be done about the education of church people, clergy and laity, in matters relating to the arts if they are to be able to enter into fruitful dialogue with artists, not only about art in churches but about art and spirituality in the world at large. For too long these two disciplines have been seen as separate and almost mutually exclusive with different aims and conflicting vocabularies. Yet each has much which it can bring to the other – art to spirituality and spirituality to art – if only they were allowed to encounter each other more frequently. When in 1977 the sculptor Edward Robinson sent a survey to 200 Anglican clergy concerning how far the development of their own religious feeling had been influenced by the visual arts only 32 bothered to reply and of these 15 said that they felt art had not influenced them at all. Based on this evidence and on his own experience Keith Walker comments that: 'it is a true but worrying fact that in the past few clergy received training in matters of artistic appreciation and many regard art as a peripheral subject not worthy of serious study' (Walker, 1996, pp. 96ff.).

Yet recent evidence suggests that a shift is taking place in the status of education in the arts for clergy and laity alike. In Salisbury Diocese, to give but one example, two of the final term's options on the Bishop's Certificate Course for 2001 related to issues in art and theology, one looking at issues in reordering churches and the other at twentieth-century stained glass. In the same year the newly ordained enjoyed a day at the workshop of the stained glass artist Tom Denny; while a Continuing Ministerial Education Day on art and spirituality was also held at Roche Court Sculpture Park where clergy were given the opportunity to discuss the theme of the day with curators and artists alike. In September 2000 the Mirfield Centre hosted a two-day residential conference on issues of art and spirituality entitled 'Teaching Souls to Fly'; while recently Durham, Gloucester and other cathedrals have had artists in residence.

What has made these educational endeavours successful is the way in which they present opportunities for Christians and artists to meet and to begin to put together a common language in which they can communicate. Each learns from the other. At Mirfield, for example, the sculptor Guy Reid, as part of 'Teaching Souls to Fly', placed his sculpture *Separation* off-centre in the south aisle of the monastic church of the Community of the Resurrection so as not to interfere with the liturgical use of the building. He was somewhat surprised when conference delegates, who included Fr Friedhelm Mennekes and Canon Keith Walker, told him that he should have centralized his sculpture under the central crossing point of the vault in the centre of the aisle and thus forced the liturgy to work around his work of art for the duration of the conference! The value of such encounters is hardly surprising. One has only to look at the achievements of artists who have worked together in the sphere of stained glass, such as John Piper and Patrick Reyntiens in England and Marc Chagall and Charles Marq in France, to see that art need not always be solitary but can also be an opportunity for mutual endeavour and collaboration at all sorts of different levels.

In commissioning a work of art communication with the artist, is as we have seen, of prime importance. Yet other people also need to be communicated with, the PCC or Church Council, the Diocesan Advisory Committee or, in the case of cathedrals, the Cathedral's Fabric Commission. Communication with the latter two bodies and with the various Amenity Societies who must be consulted are dealt with in Chapter 6. Yet this chapter would not be complete without a word on the sort of issues which must be examined when discussing a potential commission with a PCC or other Church Council or indeed with a whole church meeting. Perhaps the best example of good practice here is in the life of Walter Hussey. Whenever Hussey wished to commission a piece of art either when Rector of St Matthew's, Northampton or later as Dean of Chichester he always prepared his PCC or congregation laity well, inviting the artist to come down and speak to them directly. He also had a few trusted artistic friends upon whom he relied for connoisseur advice. He made sure that the artist, commissioning body and experts were happy with the project. And when he was assured that all these things were in place then he would stand against the conservatism of the press and others within the Church at large and tirelessly see the project through (Hussey, 1985). The key to his success was consultation and communication from beginning to end.

And this is no less true today. Faced with any project which will alter or change their church building many people will feel threatened and vulnerable and will need convincing that the project is right, that it will enhance rather than detract from the beauty of the building. This is where inviting the artist in to meet the PCC or congregation can be of such tremendous value since it may often be possible for a congregation to catch a vision from the artist which no one else can convey. It is also important that the artist comes prepared to give an idea of the size, scale and form which the work will take, not only by talking his or her ideas through but also visually by using sketches and models. This is of tremendous importance so long as it is made clear that these are only preliminary workings and that the finished project may not be exactly the same in every detail! Even more powerful in the case of a large-scale work such as a new font or pulpit is the use of a full size scale mock-up which people can walk around and look at from every angle. Church Council or congregation members will also need some idea from the artist about what the project will cost and about the time-scale envisaged, although reassurances on fundraising and debates on theology should be handled by those with the authority to do so, such as the PCC treasurer or a member of the ministry team, rather than throwing the artist to the lions!

Such meetings may be at times painful and are always time-consuming for those involved in bringing together the artists with the congregation or general public. Yet they are almost never a waste of time. For the key to a better working relationship between artists and the Church is through encounter and discussion. This is the way that subjective likes and dislikes will be overcome and the right decisions made about what sort of art will enhance a particular space. And if the congregation as well as the artist have learned something beforehand about each other's traditions and language then they will begin to explore together questions of iconography, of form and place, of colour and imagery, and so at last create together a work of fitting beauty and power. This does not mean that the work will always receive a favourable response from all who view it or live with it after it has been completed. Any church which has commissioned a piece of art may experience a wide spectrum of responses to the work both positive and negative. Interpretations cannot be easily predicted or controlled since any piece of art, if it is powerful, will make a powerful statement to those who come into contact with it as we have seen to be the case with *The Messenger*. Yet strong reactions should not deflect us if we have done our work of preparation and encounter properly for such is the task of any who dare to engage in the task of commissioning art for churches in the twenty-first century.

Yet what if there is no space or finance to commission a permanent work of art? Should the encounter between art and theology and between art and spirituality then be dismissed? Not at all. For there are many other opportunities for encounters between art and Christianity which are less ambitious. One route is to introduce art into church on a temporary basis through inviting artists to exhibit their work in the church. An exciting experiment here is the work of Father Friedhelm Mennekes in the Roman Catholic church of St Peter in Cologne. Owing to the reorganization of parish boundaries St Peter's was deemed by the authorities to be surplus to requirements and plans were made for declaring it redundant. However, Father Mennekes pleaded with the authorities to retain the church as a place where art could be exhibited, with a small congregation and regular worship. The church was stripped of most of its ornaments and artists from far and near were given wide freedom to display their work. Central to the whole scheme is a white painted triptych behind the altar of the Lady Chapel on which artists are invited to paint an image which is then displayed for the next three months. Those who have exhibited here have included Francis Bacon and George Baselitz as well as Anish Kapoor. The intention of Father Mennekes and many of the artists who have done work here is to push the boundaries of the conventional relationship between art and religion a little further. Anish Kapoor for example asked that the Rubens painting of the crucifixion of St Peter should be hung upside down. As Peter was crucified upside down the new position showed him crucified in the normal way. Then Kapoor placed a circular mirror above the altar. Many of those who saw this work did not realize at first that the Rubens painting was upside down and when they did many said that they felt foolish. Yet at one level this did not matter since the whole point is that the painting upside down symbolizes the fact that Christ came to turn the world upside down.

The worshippers at St Peter's, Cologne, at first suspicious of these developments, have now come to appreciate the art among which they live and worship. Yet there is pain and bereavement for them in this, too. For just as the worshipper is beginning to get used to a particular piece, and to incorporate it into their prayer life, it is removed at the end of its three month stay. This is all part of the process. For Mennekes would argue that art should never become comfortable and that all art, even brilliant art, loses its potency by familiarity. In this way he says we learn to love our love of the object rather than allowing the object to challenge us (Walker, 2000).

The Episcopalian Church of St Gregory of Nyssa, in San Francisco, California, is a regular venue for art exhibitions, and has fostered good relations with the wider artistic community. Indeed, a number of artists are now members of the worshipping community at St Gregory's, and one of them, Paul Mahder, a fine-art photographer, has also used the church as a studio. The context of the church, he believes, is vital to both the composition and the viewing of his work. In one series of images of the body, he used dancers as models, and has spoken of how the models, once familiar and at home with the space, were more congenial and creative in their movements than they might have been if they were photographed in a more conventional studio setting. The encounter with art in the context of a church setting is also significant. Some of Mahder's work has an explicit Christian reference, such as his *Descent from the Cross* (1999), but all of it is religiously significant, and he speaks of his work as an artist as being integral to his vocation as a Christian. But it is the setting of his exhibited work at St Gregory's, which he believes gives his work an additional religious potency, in the kind of responses it elicits from viewers. He tells of one viewer's response which could only be described as being an expression of repentance. Perhaps in the final analysis, we might say that the religious meanings and possible responses of the viewer are invited and considerably extended by the placing and viewing of a work of art in the setting of sacred space.

In England an encounter with art in churches has become possible through temporary exhibitions such as *Shape of the Century* held in and around Salisbury Cathedral as part of the 1999 Salisbury Festival and *Sculpture and the Divine* held in Winchester Cathedral in 2000. The *Art in Sacred Spaces* project has also made available contemporary works of art in several of the most southerly Anglican cathedrals. Meanwhile, *Theology for the Arts*, a University of Cambridge Research Project, has been exploring how interaction with the arts can help us explore the riches of the Christian faith in fresh and illuminating ways. As part of this project an exhibition was held in Cambridge also during 2000. Sponsored by Camfest and the Bible Society it included the work of such contemporary artists as Oliver Soskice, Charles Macksey, Richard Webb and Francis Hoyland. Finally another millenium project, *Art 2000*, invited several artists to spend time in residence at four churches in southern England. These were Tamsin Williams at Guildford (diptych of video images capturing a figure in flight), Duncan Whitley who put together a 3D sound installation at St Peter's in Brighton, Dion Ellis who also put together an audio-visual installation, this time for the baptistery at Portsmouth Cathedral, and finally Richard Wentworth who worked on a sculpture for Winchester Cathedral.

All these have been excellent short-term initiatives. The award for the most comprehensive and longest running exhibition however must go to the Methodist Art Collection. The Collection was begun in the 1960s by a Methodist layman, Dr John Gibbs, who believed that the quality of religious art and church furnishings was poor and hoped that an extensively exhibited collection would help to draw attention to the situation and encourage a more imaginative approach to the commissioning and buying of paintings, sculptures and church furnishings. Gibbs invited Douglas Wollen who was then Minister of Penarth and who also wrote regularly as an arts correspondent for *The Times* and a number of other periodicals to be the curator. Wollen collected numerous paintings by visiting a large number of exhibitions and galleries and planned an exhibition of monumental proportions to be held between July 1963 and September 1965 at a number of major galleries up and down the land. Accompanied by a subsidiary exhibition on church design and furnishings, there were 30 venues in all and attendances reached well over 100,000 (a not insubstantial figure for the time when art, and particularly religious art, was by no means as popular as it was to become by the time of the *Seeing Salvation* exhibition). After the tour the collection was kept at Kingswood School in Bath and then let out in groups of two or three paintings to various Methodist schools and colleges. In 1978 it moved to Southlands College and in 1998 to Westminster College, Oxford. The collection is available for display. Details can be found in the list of ecumenical contacts at the end of Chapter 6.

Finally, the encounter between art and theology and between art and spirituality can also be engaged with on an occasional basis through using art in worship. This may be by leading a meditation on a piece of art already in the church, such as an icon. Alternatively it is possible to use slide images. One Christmas, for an ecumenical Songs of Praise, the ministry team at St Peter's, Parkstone, in Poole, experimented with image by hanging a sheet (carefully measured and cut to size beforehand) stretched tightly across the chancel arch. Onto this we projected different images of the nativity taken from both modern and classical art and displayed one by one as the Christmas story unfolded. The effect was simple but powerful and was remembered for a long time by members of the local churches and community present at the service. With a little imagination and the willingness to plan events in advance, the possibilities of using art within worship are endless. Yet it is important too that certain basic rules are followed. First, the service must have been thought through so that the art is an integral part of the worshipping experience rather than added on seemingly as entertainment. Second, the images used should be powerful enough to speak for themselves and should not need explanation from the officiating minister. And finally those who come to worship should be given adequate time and space to reflect on a few carefully chosen images rather than being bombarded with a whole plethora of images which can only serve to irritate and confuse.

Chapter 4

Viewing Art

INTRODUCTION

Before commissioning any art for church use a number of questions need to be asked about how the work will be seen in the setting into which it will be placed. There is an intellectual question about the basic rationale for commissioning the piece of art in the first place. Then there are aesthetic questions about form, space, colour and light. All these questions would be important considerations for a work of art commissioned for any setting. Yet in the case of commissions for churches certain other issues will also need to be thought through, such as how the art will function in the building and in the liturgy and how its imagery and symbolism will work with the other symbols already in the church. And finally, too, a church may wish to ask questions, if it has gone to the trouble of commissioning a work of art, as to whether that art is fulfilling its purpose of lifting us up to God and how in that case we may use it prayerfully to the glory of God.

RATIONALE

When commissioning any work of art, and especially art for a church setting, we need to be clear as to why we are doing so. Is it because the Church Council wishes to enhance the setting of worship or draw the eye of the worshipper to a focal point in the church? Or is the work being commissioned because a parishioner or community organization has given or bequeathed money to the church to be spent on a particular project? If this is the case then the PCC or Church Council must decide if this is what they want or feel to be appropriate for the church. They must also ask themselves whether they believe the primary purpose of the donor or organization is to enhance the church setting for worship to the glory of God or whether it is to enhance the glory and status of the giver. Such questions are of course tremendously difficult and they can never be asked directly of those giving the gift. Yet it is important that Church Councils are aware that there can be a variety of motives in the mind of the donor, some of which they may not even be conscious of themselves. One question which can be asked directly and at an early stage (and which in many ways can prove to be a litmus test of the donor's motivation) is to what extent the donor wishes to be involved in the processes of commissioning the artist and in approving the design. It is, of course, to be both expected and encouraged that the donor will show an interest in the proposal and in the progress of the work. Yet it is not acceptable for the donor to try to dictate terms either to the artist or to the Church Council. If the donor begins to say that funding will only be forthcoming if all their wishes are met without question then the project is probably a non-starter from the perspective both of the artist and the church.

FORM AND SPACE

The question of form is of vital importance in any commission as it is an essential element in how the work will be viewed. Form is an elusive term which can include light, shade and shape but perhaps more importantly for present purposes it is about how each and every element of the work fits into the whole and about how the whole fits into the setting in which it is placed. It therefore also has to do with space. Form is often one of the most difficult features of a piece of art to explain but is also one of the most important.

Two examples may help us to understand what is meant by this term. The first example comes from St Matthew's Church in Northampton where, in 1944, as we have seen, Walter Hussey commissioned Henry Moore to sculpt a Madonna and Child. Photographs of this piece do not do it justice as they are almost always taken face on, at the moment, so to speak, of arrival. The piece however is to be understood as a form to be gradually approached by the visitor or pilgrim. Placed at the top of the north aisle the sculpture is visible from the church door from where the Madonna appears to beckon the worshipper towards her. At this point the Christ-Child is barely visible and is only fully encountered when the visitor arrives in front of the sculpture and encounters him face to face. A very different use of form and space can be encountered in the tapestry designed by Eleri Mills for the chapel of Poole Crematorium in Dorset, known locally and affectionately as Jacob's Ladder. The shape of the tapestry, which Eleri designed in consultation with the architect, is intended to draw the eye upwards to the lofty triangular point where the walls join the roof of the chapel at the east end. Intentionally abstract in its form and gentle in its colouring, it is intended to help mourners who face it during a service at the crematorium find inspiration and comfort in their loss. The concertina effect of the kite-tail of the tapestry can be viewed by those steeped in the Judeo-Christian tradition as representing Jacob's ladder up and down which angels ascended and descended to heaven. To many others the tapestry represents more simply a new dawn, or light, helping them through the darkness of their current sorrow and sense of loss.

Form also has to be a fundamental issue in making a decision about whether a potential new commission fits in with what is already there. Here architecture must be taken into account. How, for example, can we ensure that a contemporary commission fits in with, say, the architecture of a medieval building? Although there are no hard and fast rules about this the answer will usually lie in simplicity. Simplicity of form is perhaps the main feature that ensures that Antony Gormley's sculpture, *Sound II,* fits so beautifully into the medieval crypt with its vaulted roof at Winchester Cathedral. It is this same simplicity which William Pye has worked towards in his design for a nave font at Salisbury Cathedral. In taking for the font the shape and form of the tomb of St Osmund at the east end of the cathedral (the font is designed to fill a space near the west end of the cathedral in the centre of the nave opposite the north door) the artist's intention is to mirror a shape already well-known in the cathedral as well as to draw connections between baptism and the rising up from death to new life. His aim is that his design will reflect rather than compete with the grandeur of the cathedral itself.

There is also a question as to whether or not a commission will fit in with and complement any earlier commissions already in the church. Again this is not always an easy issue to resolve. At St Matthew's, Northampton, for example, there has been particular criticism of Malcolm Pollard's sculpture of *The Risen Christ* which many critics feel does not fit in with the earlier commissions by Henry Moore and Graham Sutherland already there. This is not an easy question to resolve. Should a great sculpture or painting from a master artist of a previous generation be allowed to dictate whether future commissions are possible or in what style they are to be executed? Surely not if the Church wishes to encourage all that is best in contemporary as well as more classical art. Perhaps again, as in the case of architecture the basic principles of simplicity of form and correct placing hold true so that art from different generations can be seen to complement and serve the whole building rather than competing with it or with each other. Finally, there are questions as to how the form of the art will serve the church building and particularly its worship. This is vital if a church is to be primarily a place of gathering for worship rather than yet another museum or gallery. And what is good art in this context? These are all questions to which we shall return in Chapter 5.

COLOUR AND LIGHT

The question of form is also related to the question of colour and light. Light, of course, is a vital element in the iconography of God within the Christian tradition where the light of God is seen as having flooded into the world in the person of Christ. This is a central feature of John's Gospel: 'and that life was the light of men' (John 1.4), and again, 'I am the light of the world' (John 8.12). The contrary side of light of course, never far from our experience, is darkness: 'and darkness covered the face of the deep' (Genesis 1.1), and 'darkness covered the whole earth from the sixth hour until the ninth hour' (Luke 23.44). Faced with this darkness ever before us it is light that helps us to see things differently and to transfigure things for us.

This theological understanding of light and its relationship to darkness caused our medieval ancestors to fill their churches with stained glass windows. They valued light because it represented all that was good and also related it to beauty. Yet in the medieval church much of this light was soft and diffused because of the colours used in the glass, especially dark blues and reds. This in its turn represented the mystery and holiness of God. It was to this sense of mystery that the reformers reacted at the Reformation. For them the best light was daylight flooding in to illuminate both word and sacrament. Thus church builders of the seventeenth and eighteenth centuries tended to fill their churches with plain windows in order that the light and beauty of nature might flood in.

Today, light, the right level of light, and how it is focused is a vital consideration in any act of worship (for more on this issue, see Chapter 5). For the same reason light, both natural and artificial, must be an important element in any artistic commission for a church. Those considering commissioning a stained glass window, for example, must consider, however intrinsically beautiful it is, whether it will let enough light into a particular church if it is habitually dark so that worship does not take place within a twilight zone. On the other hand, if too much stark light normally floods into the church it may well be a good idea to consider a stained glass window so that any harsh and cold light is both softened and diffused.

Both plain (or etched) and coloured glass can have stunning effects in the correct setting. The huge figure of Christ at Buckfast Abbey in Devon, which fills the entire eastern wall of the Blessed Sacrament Chapel, casts a stunningly beautiful and calming multicoloured light from the many facets of its blocked glass. Executed in the technique known as *dalle de verre* it was designed and executed in 1968 by Fr Charles Norris, a renowned stained glass artist and a member of the community at Buckfast. Another contemporary example of the use of coloured glass, this time of leaded glass, is at the Metropolitan Cathedral in Liverpool. Here the light which comes through the coloured glass of the lantern by John Piper and Patrick Reyntiens is designed to be seen both by day and by night. By day the daylight flooding through the lantern illuminates the whole cathedral with a diffused, coloured light focused on the altar. By night, however, light shines the other way from the illuminated cathedral into the darkened city beyond.

How contemporary stained glass has been used to enhance a medieval cathedral can be seen at Salisbury Cathedral in the Prisoners of Conscience window there. When he became dean in 1977 Sydney Evans was challenged by his friends to do something about the interior of the cathedral which 'was all glorious without but once inside you feel as if the glory has departed'. Evans realized that, given the rather dark coloured stone from which the cathedral is constructed, what was lacking from the cathedral was colour. Yet where was he to start? Eventually he decided that the east window of the cathedral, filled with a mixture of fragments of medieval and Victorian glass, which appeared almost colourless from the west end, was crucial and so the dean and chapter commissioned Gabriel Loire with experience of working with the repair and restoration of the windows at Chartres, to design a new five lancet window using medieval blues and reds. Seen at close hand the window represents in abstract form the crucifixion of Christ as the first 'prisoner of conscience' and draws the attention of the pilgrim to those in a similar plight all over the world. From afar the window provides that much needed colour for which Evans was seeking, and with its blue and red hues complements the architecture of the medieval cathedral completely.

In contrast to the light which comes through stained or coloured glass is the quality of light which passes through the plain glass windows etched by Lawrence Whistler between 1955 and 1986 at Moreton Church in Dorset. Since the church is surrounded by trees the interior would have very dark if coloured or stained glass had been chosen for the window scheme. However the plain etched glass lets in plenty of daylight and also helps to unite the church with the beautiful and natural environment which surrounds it.

Questions of lighting, both natural and enhanced, are also important when considering the suitability of a particular painting or tapestry for its proposed setting. So too are considerations of colour. The lighting and chosen background colour will both affect the way in which a commission will either stand out from or fade into the surrounding walls. Each might be appropriate, depending on the setting and intended effect. As part of its 900th anniversary celebrations in 1979 Winchester Cathedral acquired a set of banners, designed by Thetis Blacker, given by the Friends. The iconography, which represents various creational themes, is striking. Yet the greatest impact is made by the background colour of the banners, a rich gold, which both enhances and stands out from the pale golden sandstone which the cathedral builders used. The effect is both to draw the eye of the visitor or worshipper inwards towards the high altar as they stand at the end of the nave and to visually shorten the long nave so that they also feel more comfortable in what is in fact a vast space. At Salisbury Cathedral, the Lady Chapel, dominated by the Prisoners of Conscience window, posed a particular problem. Given the size of the window and its dominant colours designed to be seen from afar, how could the space be reclaimed as a chapel used daily for Morning Prayer and for the celebration of the Eucharist? The answer was to have a larger than normal altar for a mid-week celebration. For this was commissioned a modern frontal of an abstract city scene on which the light is dawning. Made in 1986 of silks and brocade hand-appliquéd over stiff interfacing, the frontal is of bright colours, designed to complement the dark blues of the window behind. The design was inspired by the *Faith in the City* Report and symbolizes the light of God coming to live there among the prisoners of each and every city.

Much simpler but also effective in its colouring is the frontal designed by Gill Bryan and Barbara Holmes for the nave altar of the reordered church of St Mary's, Wandsworth, London (1991). Bright and modern, its effective design of fish, bread and grapes, superimposed upon a divided cross, picks up the colours of the dais carpet and of the east window behind. The frontal is deliberately narrow so as not to hide the lyre-like legs of the altar made out of redundant pews from the church by another member of the congregation.

In complete contrast to these bright textiles is the altar cloth designed in 1990 by Alice Kettle for the Chapel of the Holy Sepulchre in the south aisle of Winchester Cathedral. Made as a throw or pall on which is embroidered a recumbent figure representing Christ in the tomb, the work is designed to complement and enhance the artistry and imagery of the medieval wall paintings which cover the walls of the chapel above it. The background of the cloth is silver and white, thus transferring the colours of the plasterwork into thread. There are areas both of soft pastel and of stronger colour, again to mirror the paintings with their areas both of vibrant colour and of pale image where the colour of the paint has faded back into the plaster. Gold thread is used on the cloth throughout and gives a quiet majestic glow and also picks up traces of gold on the angels' wings that are still just visible. The design is intended to become one with the medieval paintings of the chapel and because of its colouring succeeds in this. The eye is led in perfect harmony from the solitary figure of the buried Christ on the frontal through the resurrection to the Christ in majesty above.

The blending of textiles with the architecture was also an important consideration in the chosen colour scheme at Sherborne Abbey in Dorset. During the Middle Ages Sherborne suffered a serious fire which altered the colour of the remaining walls from a pale sandstone to a deep rosy pink. This has been developed as a sort of signature tune when commissioning textiles for the abbey. When a new set of hassocks were stitched they were unified by each one being given the same rose-pink background. Vestment sets have been made in the same shade and a new frontal – based on Psalm 150. These features serve to unify and harmonize the whole. A different tone, however, has recently been added in the colours of the new west window to replace the damaged Victorian window designed by Pugin from which much of the detail had flaked off. Designed by John Hayward (1997) the main colours here are strong greens and yellows. Everyone who visits here must decide for themselves whether these two schemes complement or clash with one another in the building's overall unity.

PURPOSE AND FUNCTION

Rationale, form, colour, light and space are all important issues when commissioning or viewing art. Yet perhaps the most central question when the art is an ecclesiastical commission relates to the purpose and function it will serve. Or to put it another way: How does the work enhance the life and purpose of the church, as a eucharistic community and as a place for the preaching of the word? How will it confront the worshipper/visitor with a living challenge? Does it comment in any way about the Christian life to the casual visitor? If close to the altar will it focus attention on the Eucharist or distract the worshippers with its own qualities? Two examples of recent commissions will suffice here. In 1996 the dean and chapter of Winchester Cathedral commissioned the reordering of the Swinstede Chapel as a special commemoration to St John the Evangelist and the Apostles of the Sea. The altar is carved out of a single block of wood and is flanked by two candlesticks carved to represent apostles. Simple but dramatic in its presentation it does not detract from worship. The effect of the chapel is further brought into a greater unity by the shape of the pews that are curved around the southern and western walls of the chapel like the waves of the sea. On entering the chapel the worshipper or pilgrim has a sense of being surrounded by this sea and is also led to call to mind both the waters of life and Jesus' commission to the disciples to become fishers of men. Less successful, perhaps, is the Oratory of St

Mary in St Patrick's College in Maynooth in Ireland reordered and re-orientated again in the mid-1990s. The reordering meant that the altar was now in front of two stained glass windows installed in 1937 by the Early Studios in blues and greens. Since these are placed high up on the wall they have been balanced and enhanced by the addition of a tapestry by Patrick Pye that helps to fill the east wall. Less happy below this tapestry, however, is the painting on canvas by Kim En Joong which surrounds the tabernacle by Benedict Tutty. This is both bright and abstract in design and pleasing in itself but tends to draw the eye away from the other artworks with which it shares the space. The bright and dominant colours also tend to draw the eye beyond the altar where the Eucharist is being celebrated towards the tabernacle instead and thus the central locus of the eucharistic action is lost.

IMAGERY AND SYMBOLISM

The imagery of any work of sacred art also needs to be accessible if it is to make a meaningful statement. This does not mean that all art which is used in church needs to be figurative or that the images should be child-ish, weak or facile. Hans Feibusch, writing soon after World War II, put it thus:

> Let churches be decorated by men . . . in whom there is fire to see the way. Some of our best churches are decorated with nursery emblems, golden stars, chubby angels, lilies, lambs and shepherds . . . insipid sculptures and paintings of a silly false nativity . . . one wonders in what world we live. The men who come home from war and the rest of us have seen too much evil and horror. Only the most profound moving sublime vision can redeem us. (Hussey, 1985, pp. 54–55)

Whether or not the imagery chosen is abstract or representational will vary depending on the context. Some of the best contemporary art in churches today makes use of symbol rather than image. Yet where this is so it is important that the symbols used are powerful enough to speak to the worshipper or visitor without the need for further explanation. Here we can compare and contrast the two tapestries on either side of the high altar screen at Chichester Cathedral. Before the screen, and therefore immediately behind the high altar, is a tapestry commissioned by Walter Hussey in 1966, designed by John Piper. Although bright and almost shocking in its colouring it fulfils the brief both of relieving the dull and unarresting colour of the sandstone of the cathedral and of drawing the eye of the worshipper and pilgrim up towards the high altar. It consists of a semi-abstract rendering of the Holy Trinity repre-sented by an equilateral triangle with symbols of the Father (represented by a white light), of the Son (represented by a tau cross) and of the Holy Spirit (represented by a flame-like wing superimposed upon it). This image fills the middle three of seven panels. The other four panels are filled by symbols of the four elements (earth, fire, air and water) above and of the four evangelists below. For those who have had the privilege of seeing this tapestry no explanation is needed. It speaks for itself. Less accessible, however, is the tapestry designed by Ursula Benker-Schirmer (1985) for the shrine of St Richard of Chichester which backs onto the same medieval screen. The design of this tapestry also includes a number of symbols associated with the Christian faith, a chalice to symbolize Richard of Chichester's priestly ministry, a candle to represent the glory and light of the gospel which he preached, a fig tree to represent life and a fish symbol for Christianity. Yet because of the way in which the design is carried out, as if seen through a prism of refracted light, the symbols are not immediately recognizable without a guide book in one hand and the whole comes over as a series of fragmented ideas rather than as the unified whole which is intended.

On other occasions, however, a design can become too representational and becomes akin to photo-journalism rather than art. What is meant here can be understood by comparing and contrasting two windows commissioned in commemoration of accidents at sea, one at Oystermouth on the Gower Peninsula and the other at Easton on the Portland Peninsula in Dorset (illustrated in Angus, 1984). The Oystermouth window commissioned in 1977 for the south aisle window and executed by Timothy Lewis depicts the sinking of Mumbles lifeboat with the loss of all crew in 1947. The design is a photomontage of scenes from the night of the storm and contains a great deal of graphic detail. Perhaps suitable for a secular building, in a church it fails to give a spiritual dimension to the sacrificial loss of life at sea. Very different is the window commissioned for the church of St Andrew's Avalanche on Portland Bill to commemorate the centenary of the sinking of the ships *Avalanche* and *Forest* off the coast in 1877. This window is abstract in its design, and while it conveys a sense of the wild sea and of the masts of ships, it also has a spiritual quality. The 106 men, women and children who lost their lives in the disaster are commemorated in the clear glass bubbles that are part of the design. These bubbles appear to rise up through the water and remind us that within the Christian message, where there is disaster there is also the promise of life everlasting with God.

BEAUTY

Another consideration in art for church use relates to the question of beauty. Like questions relating to form, questions of beauty are extremely elusive to explain or quantify. One can strangely often identify beauty more easily when it is lacking rather than when it is present. The worshipper or pilgrim is here, to a large extent, reliant on the artists themselves having an understanding of what beauty is about. For without this understanding a work can be decorative or pleasing, but will remain rooted in earthly rather than heavenly things, an object with feet of clay rather than with wings of fire.

Within church commissions beauty raises what we might call religious art, work illustrating a belief or doctrine translated into stone or wood, glass or paint, into sacred art, which lifts the worshipper or pilgrim into a different and higher realm of enraptured contemplation above sense and reason. For this reason sacred art is also always more than pictorial and representational because it also contains something of truth and integrity (Tillich, 1987, p. 207).

If we are to attempt to quantify it, beauty can be said to be related to form, to the fittingness of a thing to itself, of all its individual parts to themselves and to each other and to the whole and of the whole to all things. To Robert Grosseteste, thirteenth-century bishop of Lincoln, such beauty was a microcosm of God's relationship to the universe. 'God is supremely simple, supremely concordant and supremely appropriate to himself' (Eco, 1986, p. 48). For C. S. Lewis, beauty is a mirror that sends us back to our own desire for goodness. There may perhaps be something of a desire for possession in all this; the desire for the thing that we are contemplating to become part of us. But there is also a desire for it to change us.

> We do not merely want to see beauty. We want something else which can hardly be put into words; to be united with the beauty we see, to pass into it and to receive it into ourselves, to bathe in it and to become part of it. For if we take the imagery of Scripture seriously; if we believe that God will one day give us the morning star and call us to put on the splendour of the sun then we may surmise that both the ancient myth and modern poetry may be very near the truth of prophecy. At present we are on the wrong side of the door. We discern freshness and purity but it does not make us fresh and pure. We cannot mingle with the splendours that we see. But all the leaves in the New Testament are rustling with the rumour that it will not always be so. Some day God willing we shall get in. (Lewis, 1993, p. 96)

Beauty then is that which in a work of art, lifts us up heavenward, that which transforms or transfigures our souls if only for a moment towards a glimpse of the greatest truth, that is God. Discerning beauty is not easy from illustrations. One needs to stand before a work, to contemplate it, to breathe it and be drawn into it to experience its beauty for oneself. And this, in its turn, may lead to prayer.

VIEWING ART PRAYERFULLY

Today in our liturgies and in our Bible reading we have come to think of prayer so often as involving word and intellect rather than senses or being. Yet to confine prayer in this way is to impoverish it and to deprive ourselves of those moments of transformation and understanding when heaven's gates seem to be rolled back so that we might glimpse the divine more clearly. For sometimes our prayer needs to be beyond words, an outpouring of thankfulness and praise or an opening up of the spirit to simply be, for a moment, with God. Yet in this busy world reaching that place set apart becomes ever more difficult. For some finding that place of 'being' with God can be focused through listening to music. For others it will become a reality when they look at a beautiful sunset or a starlit sky. And for an increasing number of people it becomes a possibility too when they look prayerfully at a piece of art which moves them.

Paul Tillich wrote movingly of his own first encounter with God through art in his seminal work *On Art and Architecture*. He describes how a picture book copy of Botticelli's *Madonna with Singing Angel* had helped him to retain his sanity during the First World War. After the war he decided to go and visit the painting for himself in Berlin. Later he was to write:

> Gazing up at it I felt a state approaching ecstasy. In the beauty of the painting there was beauty itself. It shone through the colours of the painting as the light of day shines through the stained glass windows of a medieval church. As I stood there bathed in the beauty which the painter had envisioned so long ago something of the divine source of all things came to me. I turned away shaken. That moment has affected my whole life, given me keys for the interpretation of human existence, brought vital joy and spiritual truth. I compare it with what is usually called revelation in the language of religion. (Tillich, 1987, p. 235)

What Tillich encountered as he stood before Botticelli's painting was a sense of God's presence with him and a sense also of the truth and joy and yearning which are at the very heart of prayer. For each of us there may be a special painting, sculpture or piece of music which helps us to open ourselves to God. If so, and if we know what that piece of music, painting or sculpture is, then that is where we need to begin. Yet for many others the search is still on. They yearn for an encounter with God which is beyond words but do not know where to start.

The eastern Churches have a much better understanding of this type of prayerful encounter than we have had in the West at least since the Reformation. In this they have been helped by the use of icons. As we have already seen in Chapter 1 the purpose of the icon is not to provide an object for worship in the painting or image itself for that would be idolatry. Rather the purpose of the icon is to help the worshipper through veneration to focus themselves anew, to set aside earthly things for a moment and thus, being transformed, to draw into a closer relationship with Christ himself (Begbie, 2000, p. 83). In this the one who seeks to pray is helped by several features of the process by which icons are prepared. First, before he begins to paint an icon the artist has already prepared himself by fasting and prayer for the task in hand. The icon painting itself is also an act of prayer. And so when worshippers come to use that icon to pray they are part of a much wider circle of prayer which encompasses and surrounds them in their own endeavours to draw near to the Godhead. Second, the icon painter does not have a free hand to do as he wishes when painting the icon. There are certain styles and forms which must be observed, laid down by the Orthodox Church. These are part of a sacred trust, believed to originate from God himself. This means that the icon when completed will be a much more stylized work of art than we are used to encountering in the West. This has the effect of freeing the icon to help focus worship as the eye is not distracted by details of interpretation and expression imposed by the artist himself. Finally, those venerating icons are also drawn in, in many instances, by the eyes of the figure of Christ or the saints; because of the way in which they have been painted, they engage and follow our own eyes throughout the time of prayer.

Given the power of the icon it is hardly surprising that icons are being used more and more as aids to worship in western churches as well as in the East. In Britain perhaps the most outstanding set of icons in a western church are those which now adorn the reverse of the reredos behind the high altar at Winchester Cathedral. This reredos originally had a number of niches filled in the Middle Ages with statues. When these were destroyed at the Reformation the screen was left bare until recently the decision was taken to fill each of the central niches with an icon. Although this area of the cathedral has always been something of a walkway for visitors traversing the east end, there is happily still room for the worshipper or pilgrim to stand in front of their chosen icon to pray. This is not the case in all churches with icons. In some the icons can be found placed above a doorway or high up on a wall where they can only serve a decorative purpose and can never be used as they were intended, as a tool for contemplation and as an aid to prayer.

Chapter 5

The Art of Worship

In the last two chapters we have looked at ways in which art might be used both to inform and enhance worship. Yet all this can only ever be true if we are also conscious of a fundamental premise that worship itself is art, a creative expression of our worship and praise of God. Public worship therefore, if it is to be worthy of the name must be planned and executed just as carefully as if one were Michelangelo painting the ceiling of the Sistine Chapel. For worship is only true worship if it is about the offering of the very best that we can do and give to Almighty God.

For most people the very word 'church' refers to a building, the place where Christians gather for worship, and despite our protestations and attempts to explain that 'the people are the church', this is how the word church is most frequently used and understood. Strictly speaking, the term *ecclesia* denotes a convocation, people called together to be a corporate body, and the reason they are called together is to offer worship. In an earlier chapter we have shown that the church as a physical building has been regarded as more than a necessary shelter, or even a convenient meeting place, but a place which from the time of the earliest 'church-houses' was deliberately adapted for the specific activity of worship. As such, the physical building itself constituted part of the very fabric of our meeting with God, and of the complex symbolic transactions between God and humanity. In this chapter we are seeking to tease out further the relationship between art and worship, and to show how worship itself might be seen as an art form.

Our starting point might be the apparent common ground suggested by the liturgical theologian, Aidan Kavanagh, and the sculptor, Barbara Hepworth. Kavanagh asserts that the church and its worship are located in the rough and tumble landscape in which people discover and quarry meaning and purpose in their lives, and intriguingly suggests that this is an artistic enterprise (Kavanagh, 1984, p. 139). Barbara Hepworth once exclaimed that 'all true works of art are an act of praise'. She had been profoundly affected by the peculiar blend of industrial and rural landscape of her native West Yorkshire, and in this landscape saw the effects of natural erosion and how it revealed its rocky substructure. Interestingly her own work, whether sculptured stone, or carved wood, was shaped by the texture, grain and colouring of the material with which she worked. In this she showed a preoccupation with 'form', and a number of her works were simply given the title 'Form'. Her artistic vision was a 'seeing in depth', a seeing, that is, beyond the surface appearance to the underlying form of things. Hepworth believed that uncovered form, in the finished and polished work of art, was indicative of the very force of life which lay behind the inanimate matter of the physical world.

Since the time of Gregory Dix, liturgical theologians, too, have been preoccupied with seeking to discern the shape, or form of the liturgy, of looking behind the surface text to the form, or structure of the liturgy. Perhaps Dix was too easily seduced by the specific notion of a fourfold shape, but in seizing upon the notion he unintentionally drew our attention to the question of form as it unfolds in an actual act of worship. More contemporary work in critical theory invites us to look beyond the surface of a text in order to engage with its deep structures, to read, as it were, the underlying grammar of the text in order to see how it actually works. The first to apply this in the field of liturgical studies was Robert Taft in his study of the development of the Byzantine Liturgy (Taft, 1984). Taft applied the tools of structural analysis to historical liturgical texts and demonstrated that the development of liturgical forms was, as it were, uneven, with so-called 'soft-points' attracting embellishment in order to compete with the pristine elements in the primitive forms of the Byzantine Liturgy. In seeking the 'deep structures' Taft attempted to construct an understanding of how the elements of the liturgical text being investigated might actually work (cf. Taft, 1984, p. 152). Such avenues of enquiry are salutary, especially in a time such as ours when liturgical revision has been running at fever pitch, and we so readily equate liturgy with a text, and worse, come to regard worship as the reading of an approved and authorized printed service. For liturgy, of course, is much more than text.

A wider view was proposed by the Orthodox theologian, Alexander Schmemann, who stressed the importance of seeing liturgy as a whole worshipping event and experience. More recently, Kevin Irwin in *Context and Text* construed an understanding of the *lex orandi* (rule of prayer) not as identified with any particular liturgical text (which are invariably shaped by the *lex credendi* – rule of belief), but with the kinds of prayer which constitute an unfolding liturgical event. In this, Irwin comes close to locating the form, or underlying structure of the Church's liturgy.

The implications drawn by Irwin undoubtedly require further scrutiny, but our concern is to tease out further the premise that it is within the 'rite', or what in eastern terms is called the 'Ordo', defined as the whole performed event of worship, that we might locate the deep structures of the liturgy. These structures undoubtedly influence the shape of the liturgy, but they should not be simply equated with it. We might compare these deep structures to the movements in a symphony, in which each movement, though being discrete, might surface and occur in the phrasing of another. Furthermore, as with the movements in a symphony, so the structures of a liturgical rite give form to all that intentionally happens in that act of worship, and give it its dynamic flow and rhythm.

The cumulative effect of these considerations leads to the view that the structure of worship pertains more to its nature as event, rather than in the shape of its component parts, however they might be categorized. In order to validate such a view, one would need to point to certain elements in an act of worship which might be indicative of the deep structures to which we have already alluded. Here one might think, for example, of:

- the act of gathering (with the invocation of the triune God reconstituting those assembled as an *ecclesia*) and the dismissal (with its accent upon the commissioning and empowering of the Church dispersed in the world);
- the declaiming of the word and confession (ostensibly, the confession of sin as well as the confession of faith), and forms of petition and praise;
- the symbols and symbolic gestures of offering (such as the public mutual declaration of love in marriage; the presentation of a child for baptism; presentation of the gifts of bread and wine for the Eucharist), and the gratuitous divine donation of grace in sacramental celebrations.

The pairings sketched out here are merely suggestive and require a more systematic elucidation, but by way of qualification one should say that the divine initiative is always to be seen to be primary, and that the range of liturgical responses, whether in the form of the praying of a liturgical text (of whatever time or place), or the making of a ritual gesture, are to be regarded as being secondary. Such responses correspond to what is described in musical terms as counterpoint, in this instance a counterpoint, as it were, to the divine art of creation and redemption. In other words one might say that in all the aspects of a worship event, in the saying, silences, singing and doing, there is a reciprocity, an expected answering response on the part of the worshippers, which in some sense completes the art of worship and makes it a truly dialogical and a participatory event. At this point, one might recall what the sculptor Naum Gabo wrote in a letter to the art historian and critic, Herbert Read, to the effect that a piece of art was in some sense incomplete until it was engaged by, and responded to by the viewer (Robinson, 1987).

Similarly, the liturgy is complete not when it attains the status of a text for authorized usage, but when it is performed as a vehicle for the Church's corporate prayer. Yet one must also be cautious in using the term 'performance' in this context, not least because the celebration of a rite is not restricted to those with obvious liturgical roles, such as ordained ministers, readers, cantors and musicians. There is, of course, a differentiation of roles and distinctive ministries within an ordered Church, and although what pertains to one does not always pertain to another, all those, ordained and lay, who have a particular role to play in an act of worship should never intrude like overbearing personalities giving a solo performance, but should play their part in a way which facilitates the engagement of the whole gathered community in the act of worship. For the liturgy is a corporate action, and one which invites and requires the response of all those who have gathered to what is heard, said, sung and seen, within the worship environment. Worshippers, of course, respond to an act of worship in various ways and at various levels, and one should not presuppose, as seemingly happens, that the only significant way in which an individual worshipper participates in an act of worship is to actually say or do something. Such a presupposition is frequently reinforced by some contemporary styles of worship and has evidently raised some misleading expectations. The fact is that there are many different levels at which a worshipper might respond to the setting and the event of worship, and one of these ways might well be in the keeping of an appropriate stillness and receptive silence (Irvine, 2001).

Taken as a whole event, there is a considerable range of stimuli within an act of worship and a great deal of it is aural. Words are spoken and declaimed in the vocal prayers, scripture readings, the sermon, and sung in hymns and psalmody, but in all these words, more is said than is spoken or sung, for each offers an invitation to enter into a deeper spiritual dialogue with God in Christ: 'The Spirit and the Bride say, "Come." And let everyone who hears say, "Come."' (Revelation 22.17). But the impact of ocular stimuli can be just as significant. The dialogical structure of Psalm 27.8 implies that the visual too can be an invitation to a deeper engagement on the part of the worshipper: '"Come," my heart says, "seek his face!" Your face, Lord, do I seek.'

We should come to worship, then, with the intention to participate, and with the expectation that we might well be engaged at a profound level of our being. The church building is a 'laboratory of the Spirit', and ought to be a place where our attention is heightened and arrested by its very ambience. But what exactly is the worshipper responding to? Is it more than the mood, or feel of the building? At a very significant level, the worshipper responds to what we shall present as the 'arts of worship', and it precisely these arts which facilitate what we might call the dialogical character of worship. For an act of worship is not solely a human activity, but the covenanted locus of our encounter with the triune God, who is the hidden and silent actor in the performance of the 'holy theatre' of worship. It is God who moves among us, who speaks his word, who reveals his glory and donates his grace in the sacramental gifts through all the changing moods, movements, and moments of an unfolding act of worship.

Worship then can, and should, be the occasion when we might catch a vision of something greater than ourselves, an experience which some-times poses a searching question as to who one is, and where one truly belongs. But significantly, in all this one is never left alone, left without companions for the journey. For although the range of possible indi-vidual responses on the part of a worshipper are incalculable, there is one effect which can and should be reckoned with, and that is the cor-porate effect of worship, the heightening and intensifying of a sense of being a part of the body of Christ: 'for we being many are one bread, one body, because we all participate in the one bread' (1 Corinthians 10.17). Indeed, all that happens during an act of worship conspires to inculcate a sense of being incorporated within a single offering of prayer and praise. The Lord's Prayer, the very model of all Christian prayer and praise, begins in the first person plural, '*Our* Father', remind-ing us that each worshipper's voice is to blend with a whole company of voices, the very praying body of Christ in any given time and place. Likewise, in an act of worship, each worshipper is caught up in the rhythm of the liturgy, and all find their part not as mere spectators, but as participants. For this reason our attendance is crucial, not just our physical being there, but the level of attention which each worshipper should bring to an act of worship.

Those who have particular responsibilities in conducting worship need to take special care to prepare themselves and to maintain their attention throughout the celebration. They are to be attentive not only to what they say, and how they say it, but also sensitive to what their movements around the church, and their posture during those parts of a service led by others might communicate to the members of the congre-gation. Sitting with one's legs crossed in a position which is directly visible to the congregation during the reading of scripture does not really signal to other worshippers that this moment in the celebration is the time for attentive listening! The one who presides at the liturgy is rather like a conductor, enabling each person within the worshipping community to play their particular part at the appropriate moment, and has the task of seeking to orchestrate the various parts of the liturgy so that it is experienced as a unified whole, a corporate offering directed to God. The president has the responsibility to set the appropriate pace, tone and mood of the particular celebration, and this best happens when the president has an informed feel for how the distinctive movements and moments of a given celebration are part of a unified whole, a sense that is, of the form of the liturgy determined by its deep structures. This informed sense of the form of a liturgical celebration, an appreciation that 'in its wholeness liturgy is an event wherein actual occasions, moments are interrelated in some determinative shape or fashion' (Hoche-Mong, 1976), is precisely what the art of liturgical presidency consists of.

But what of the worshippers themselves? How and in what ways might they contribute to the art of worship? One might begin to address this question by considering an unfinished painting by the English visionary artist Stanley Spencer, entitled *Christ Preaching at Cookham Regatta*. The painting locates the figure of Christ in the midst of a social gathering. A number of the figures on this wide canvas are simply painted in outline. The fully painted figures reveal a vibrant sense of movement and activity, and thereby indicate what the full form of the painting might have been. But the painting was unfinished, and this brings us to the finer point of the comparison, namely, that an act of worship is also incomplete until that moment when the people take their place and begin to play their part in the act of worship. The people who gather for worship correspond to the sketched outlines on the canvas of Spencer's unfinished painting, and all that they bring and express in an act of worship gives particular colour and local texture to it. The needs, gifts and concerns which each worshipper brings to an act of worship, and which are expressed in the appropriate moments of the unfolding act of worship, such as the prayers of penitence, intercession, the acts of offering, praise and adoration, constitute what in artistic terms we might call the 'expressive form' of an act of worship. The inherent form of the liturgy, the shape determined by the deep structures of the liturgy, corresponds to the means whereby God achieves, as it were, the restoration of the divine art. But before we treat this subject, we must consider how that form is revealed in the various art forms utilized in liturgical celebrations.

Our contention then is that a liturgical celebration is itself a complex art-form, of both divine and human making, and as such it is not surprising to see that a range of different artistic forms have been adopted and utilized by the Church in its worship. These art-forms are intrinsic to the very nature and purpose of liturgy, and it would be too restrictive and limiting to see them as mere decoration, or as an optional aesthetic enhancement and beautification of worship. Thus Aidan Kavanagh draws the conclusion that 'the liturgical scholar who is illiterate in the several arts can never know his or her subject adequately' (Kavanagh, 1984, p. 139). Perhaps in this instance Kavanagh demands too much, but given the nature and purpose of worship it is not unreasonable to say that all who exercise the responsibility of planning and conducting worship, and those who have the care of the Church's fabric, ought to at least appreciate how worship needs the arts to exhibit its form and to release its formative effect.

Here, we need to speak of the arts in plural, and among the various artistic forms and languages serving the liturgy, we might draw attention to the following areas of interaction between worship and the arts.

ARCHITECTURE, DESIGN, STRUCTURE AND FABRIC OF CHURCH BUILDINGS

Each architectural style, from domed space, through baroque, to the functional utilitarian buildings of the 1960s, encapsulates particular theological convictions about the meaning of worship, but such concrete definition invariably constrains the style of liturgical celebration which can take place in that particular building. Disasters in reordering, however defensible the theological agenda, often come down to the fact that what is possible in one building is not immediately transferable to another. As the building itself is more than a utilitarian setting for worship, its design and the materials used for its construction should ideally articulate the multiple meanings of worship. The scale of a church building is also significant, as it demands, for a number of reasons, an amplitude of space (Rouet, 1997, p. 118). For a church is a place of encounter, a place where there ought to be sufficient space for one to meet with another, and for each to be met by the Other. There also needs to be room for the stranger, or occasional visitor, as well as sufficient space and seating for the gathering of the regular congregation. But this rarely means that the whole area of the nave needs to be filled with seating. Furthermore, a church needs to be a resonant space, in order to amplify the word and the voice of praise.

The internal decoration of the building must be in sympathy with the architectural lines and mood of the building. The colour scheme should highlight the architectural lines, and reveal the texture of the materials with which it is constructed, and provide an element of warmth. The decoration need not be in pastel or subdued colours, but one must be aware that an overdecorated building can create the impression of being a buzzing and cluttered space, and might possibly detract from the building's essential meaning and purpose, which is to focus and direct the attention of the worshippers to God.

The lighting of a building is also a crucial factor. The building requires good illumination, both natural and artificial. There ought always be some source of natural light, through wall windows, lanterns, or other roof lighting, to remind worshippers that the created order should impinge upon our worship. Natural light, filtered through clear, tinted, or coloured glass, gives a certain play of light within the building, and to have such a play of shadows and light within a building through the changing hours of the day and the changing seasons, can forcefully suggest, at least subliminally, that time spent in prayer and praise in that building is none other than the very sanctification of time itself. The electric light fittings should be discreet, and it is desirable that they should be separately controlled with dimmer switches in order that one can create a variability of illumination in the different parts of the building. Controlling the intensity of light, and the facility for spotlighting particular spaces, features and fittings, can assist in drawing the worshippers' attention to the changing areas of liturgical action, or foci of devotion, during the course of an act of worship. Having such controlled lighting affects the mood of the building, and this again reminds us that good interior lighting is not the same as flooding an area with artificial light. Such lighting is often harsh, and the tendency to overlight modern buildings is best resisted in churches. There obviously needs to be sufficient directed light to enable worshippers to see and read, but it is also desirable to create some shadows in the corners and arches of the building. A good lighting scheme will also provide some shadows in the building, and therefore will suggest to worshippers that the place where we gather for worship is the very place where we are drawn to the light, the very light of the risen Christ. Thus, a worship space needs its unlit corners, its darker spaces, not least for those who, for whatever reason, are feeling vulnerable or overwhelmed by the darkness of depression. After all, it is from the shadows that we can best see the light, and for those who are enlightened at the baptismal font, the light of Christ which dawns with the declaration of forgiveness is experienced as a ray of healing love and mercy, and not as an intrusive and blinding searchlight leaving one feeling vulnerable and exposed.

KINETIC ARTS

The kinetic arts are also arts which the liturgist and all involved in the conduct of worship should be especially aware of. In considering the positioning of furniture and fittings in a building, one has again to be sensitive to the use of space and have an eye to the interior visual land-scape. Ideally the whole area should be used, with sufficient margins of space kept between fittings and furniture. This will allow for easy and deliberate movement from one part of the church to the other. There is no reason why the various focal points of the liturgy need to be located along the same axis at the front of the building. Where we locate the font, reading desk, or lectern, and the altar, is significant for the dynamic of liturgical celebrations. Each needs to have a certain prom-inence and visibility in order to maximize the worshippers' particip-ation in the celebration. But this is best done by setting them in their own defined space. Ideally the font should be placed at some distance from the altar, such as the traditional west end of the building near the entrance, in order to allow for the kind of processional movement which is integral to the form of a liturgy which celebrates the Christian's pilgrimage 'on the way'. Again, the lectern, from which the scriptures are read and the sermon preached, might well be positioned among the people, not only to give some semblance of the congregation being gathered around the word, but also to signal that the words declaimed and heard need to be translated into the actual lives lived by the people of God. The altar should be visible to all in the building. Indeed, an altar in the traditional location in the east end of the building is a vital reminder that the Lord who makes himself known in the breaking of bread has 'gone before us', and summons us beyond where we presently find ourselves. An altar set in the round might well signal the 'divine in our midst', but the danger for the congregation is that they might come to think that the transcendent is contained within their circle. Again, the interior design needs to signal clearly an openness to the transcen-dent, and so a closed circle of chairs is best avoided.

PERFORMING ARTS

By this we mean the performance of liturgical texts, ritual acts, the use of the voice in prayer and song, and in the making of music. Compared with the rather spare and bald language of *The Alternative Service Book 1980*, the texture of language of the so-called modern language services in *Common Worship* exhibits a richness in imagery, resonance and rhythm, and a greater care and sensitivity is required of those who 'perform' these rich texts. Some of these texts, such as canticles, thanks-giving prayers and so on, can, and if possible should, be sung. The sound of praise, after all, is song. The soaring solo voice of the president singing the Preface at the Eucharist should help the people to 'lift up their hearts and minds' to God, and the singing of parts of the service by the whole congregation can intensify the sense of their being a corporate body together. Music, because of its associational character, can add to what the people who gather for a liturgical celebration actually bring to that act of worship. A particular hymn or piece of music might well, for instance, trigger memories of particular occasions, such as weddings or funerals, and when memories occur, the emotional history and needs of the whole person can be opened up and made accessible to the influence of that particular celebration. This is especially the case with the singing of hymns. Music can inspire, disturb, uplift and move the heart. It is also a primary language of worship, and possibly the purest form of language to voice the transcendent. As such music could, as in the Lutheran tradition, play a greater part in our worship, rather than simply happen to cover movement, such as when a collection is taken, or the congregation is gathering or leaving the building. Music, whether instrumental, or vocal, can also complete the architecture, and fill the building with sound. Its changing tonal hue can effectively draw out the various moods of the particular moments of an unfolding liturgical celebration itself. Like words, music too, as sound in time, can lead worshippers into moments of receptive silence, especially when the sound rises to a peak and then dies away, accentuating the silence and a corporate receptivity to that Word, which speaks most often in silence. Silences in worship, as we have already said, are deliberate and purposeful, and it is important that the whole time of worship is not filled with words and music.

VISUAL ART

The principles guiding the use and placing of visual art have already been set out in an earlier chapter, but perhaps one might reiterate the importance of *good* art being placed in the setting for worship. But what might count as good art in this particular context? Two criteria will suffice here. The first, already alluded to in Chapter 4, is that the art placed in a liturgical setting must be congruent with all that happens there. The Lutheran liturgical theologian, Gordon Lathrop, though offering little on the subject of art and worship, has argued that the visual arts placed in church must be transparent to the central signs of the liturgical gathering, and must not attract attention to themselves (G. Lathrop, 1993, p. 169). One suspects that a subservient and limited view of the function of art in worship underlies this stricture. However, Lathrop's work does support the view that the art placed in a church ought to be congruent with the purpose and function of the church building as a place of worship. The context is crucial, and consideration needs to be given to where works of art are placed in the church. The issues here are not the same as those with which one would work if one was considering where to hang a work of art in a gallery. And the immediate question would not be to find the best place for the piece to viewed, but the place where it might best interact with, and complement, the liturgical action. An excellent example of the appropriate placing of art is Hans Feibusch's painting of the *Baptism of Christ*, which hangs on the wall behind the font in Chichester Cathedral. Here the painting undoubtedly adds to what is celebrated in that part of the building. An often cited work, but one which on this score is not especially well sited, is the Graham Sutherland *Crucifixion*, which hangs on the south wall of the south transept of St Matthew's Church, Northampton. It is an extraordinarily powerful painting, but as a friend remarked, it is easily overlooked by being placed in an area which, liturgically and devotionally speaking, is a rather dead space. The new incumbent is aware of this, and is now using that area for the veneration of the cross during the liturgy on Good Friday. The placing of good art in church, it seems, requires both a liturgical as well as an aesthetic sensibility.

The two examples cited were the work of two internationally renowned artists, but one must stress that good art is not always exorbitantly priced, or beyond the financial means of a parish or community. But whatever the cost, the crucial thing is that the art is well crafted and skilfully executed, and this point brings us to the second of our criteria of good art, namely, that it must be well made from good materials. Here, one might think of Guy Reid's *Madonna and Child* sculpture in St Matthew's Church, Westminster, which has received critical attention in the media and Church press. It is a work of considerable craftsmanship, skilfully carved in lime wood, and being unpainted, reveals the integrity and beauty of the natural material. Incidentally, the commissioning of a piece like this would not be beyond the financial means of a large parish. But, alas, churches all too often take the easy option and purchase factory-produced plaster statues, which border on being kitsch.

Finally then, good art is durable and never ephemeral. It is good to employ the skills of local artists, to insist on the use of good materials, and an insistence on good craftsmanship does not exclude the artistic work arising from the culture of a specific locality. The only point at issue here is that we utilize the best skills and materials. For as the name implies, worship is the giving and the showing of what is considered to be of worth, and to serve this expressed purpose only the best will do. The art needs to be seeming and fitting. A garishly painted plaster Madonna and Child might well convey a religious sentiment, but can it convey the weight of the mystery of the incarnation? The installation of representational art, especially of a devotional kind, in an ecclesiastical setting is always a risk. In matters of devotion, sentiment can easily, and in fact often does, override wider questions of aesthetic value, and of whether the devotional responses of its viewers are appropriate to, and congruent with, our theological understanding of that which it represents. This is not to say that sentiment does not have a legitimate place in our responses to religious devotional art. It certainly does and should. But the point in question here is whether the artefact, whether painting or sculpture, leads the viewer to a deeper appreciation and apprehension of the religious truth it portrays and evokes, or whether its effect might lead to a trivialization, or worse, distortion of Christian experience, both of God and of the realities of human birth, motherhood, life and death.

Our overriding principle bearing on the placing of art in church is that it should be appropriate and fitting, and this applies to furniture, fabrics and fittings as much to visual art. Ideally, each item, though not necessarily homogenous in style, material and design, should form part of an integrated whole, constituting, as it were, the 'holy theatre' of the interaction between the human and the divine. But this does not mean that everything must be of the same artistic style, or belong to the same stylistic period. The point is that the visual arts, decoration, furnishings and fittings in a church should form an ensemble, in which each item might take up a feature of another, and contrive to draw the worshipper into the very art of God. A modest example of such an ensemble, where various devotional objects and decoration of different style and media form a harmonious whole, is the Church of St Alban the Martyr, built in the early 1930s. St Alban's is set in a maze of Victorian terraced housing in East Oxford. Its architect, Lawrence Dale, prevailed upon Eric Gill to design a set of stations of the cross, and the first nine of these 14 stations were engraved in Gill's workshop before his death in 1940. The theme of Christ's passion, of suffering and self-giving, depicted in the stations is taken up with the red painted lines and the traditional emblems of Christ's passion (such as the cockerel, Judas' money bag, the dice, etc.) painted on either side of wooden roof beams. In 1997 a stained glass artist, Vital Peters, was commissioned to design and make a window, which was to be installed in a refurbished chapel. The window was to be set in the east wall of the church, above the altar, and at the same eye level as the cross beams crossing the width of the nave. The new arched window mimicked the Romanesque-style external windows set in the north and south walls of the church, and although its design was abstract and geometrical, with a number of different textured glass shapes, the artist was careful to pick out and include in the new window the colours of the passion emblems in the body of the church. So both artistically and theologically, it was part of a unified thematic whole.

A great many churches are architecturally multilayered and contain fittings and art from a range of different periods. Where this is the case, it gives a historical depth to the building and reminds the congregation that they are linked to previous generations of worshippers who gathered in that building. The very building, then, can serve as a witness to that 'communion of saints' which transcends all time and locality. However, whether the church is a historical building, or a modern one, its architecture, its arts, and the worship offered there should be all of a piece, and serve to evoke and express the God 'who wills to approach and to be approached' (Brown, 1990, p. 125). And when one considers how the architecture and the art of the building might function, one is reminded that it can work at various levels simultaneously: it can function pedagogically, it can be decorative, challengingly inspirational even, but above all, it can and should work in harmony with all that happens in an act of worship. Without doubt, the arts can be a powerful vehicle for engaging the worshipper in the mystery which is celebrated in the liturgy, and which becomes accessible to the worshipper through the unfolding structures of an act of worship. At this level the liturgical arts might be described as participatory, as was undoubtedly the case, for example, with the mosaics of the baptism of Christ in the Baptistries of Ravenna (Wharton, 1987). It certainly can have the power to elicit appropriate responses from the worshipping viewer at every level of their being, their thinking, feeling, and even bodily posture. For in an act of worship it is possible for every sense to be engaged, and for our responses to be elicited through thought, emotion and bodily gesture. The power of the liturgical arts, then, consists in their power to elicit appropriate responses from the worshipper and to mediate the very mystery which is declaimed and celebrated in the liturgy. This latter point was made by Abbot Herwegen and Odo Casel, of the Rhineland Abbey of Maria Laach, who viewed the various arts used in worship as constituting a total artform, what they called a *Gesamtkunstwerk*, and which, they claimed, mediated and made accessible the divine reality encountered in worship (see Irvine, 1993, pp. 102f. and 114f.).

Some might consider the so-called mystery theology of Odo Casel as being too abstract and neatly schematic, and to be some distance from their own experience of worship. But a compatible view has been suggested more recently by Gordon Lathrop, who again underlines the role of art in revealing the very structures of worship with which we began our exploration in this chapter. Lathrop argues that art most clearly serves a Christian purpose when it helps to reveal the very structure of Christian worship: 'cultural symbols – music, ceremony, environmental arrangement, gesture, vestments, arts – will come to

Christian purpose most clearly as they serve the flow of those very simple ancient patterns of Baptism and Eucharist which belong to their origins' (Lathrop, 1999, p. 202). His suggestive phrase of 'the flow of ancient patterns of Baptism and Eucharist' seems to imply the underlying form and deep structures of the liturgy, which we might take as the tools of God's art.

At each point in our discussion we have attempted to show that the dynamic of worship is a double movement, a movement flowing both ways, as it were, from God to humanity (the workings of divine grace in incorporating, and sustaining us as Christ's body, through baptism and Eucharist), and from humanity to God (in the bearing and bringing of human concerns, and the material circumstances of people's lives into the arena of God's transformative action through our presence, prayer and the materiality of sacramental symbols). In this sense, worship is both the unfolding in time and place of God's redemptive work, the liberating of creation from its bondage to decay, through the manifesting of the sons and daughters of God (Romans 8.21), and the voicing of praise and thanksgiving, the articulation of human need, and the means of offering ourselves, our souls and bodies, in union with Christ. Such a double, reciprocal movement, realizes what might be taken as the liturgical formation of worshippers, but this too can be accounted for in wider artistic terms.

In this regard we might take our cue from the fourth-century eastern theologian, Basil the Great who, in commenting on the divine work of creation, described the world as God's studio, and thereby implied that God's creatures were his art. It is our contention that the considerations we have made in this chapter might lead us to adopt and apply this analogy to the arena of worship, and speak of the very church building as that studio of God in which he is seeking to renew his creation, and to form those who worship into 'the likeness of Christ'. For those who in Paul's telling expression 'manifest the life of Christ' are of God's making, are God's work of art. It is as though the divine grace, mediated through various arts of worship, effects our 'remaking', our transformation from 'one degree of glory to another'. Such a pattern of redemptive restoration is already modelled in that earlier paradigm of the transactions of worship encapsulated in Hebrew psalmody. Psalms 48.8, 9 and 66.4 express invitations to both hear and to *see*. What is seen and heard by the worshippers is presumably some visual representation of God's saving presence, but interestingly the apparent effect of seeing such a representation is that they come to reflect in their own countenance something of the transfiguring splendour of God's saving presence. The invitation to come and worship also holds the promise of transformation. For those who are drawn to the courts of God will be blessed, and fulfilled, not by any self-expression, or self-realization on their own part, but by the Creator's gift of his own goodness, holiness, and beauty. To be faced with such transforming goodness, holiness and beauty is to be faced by what is most fully and really real, as opposed to what might be more immediately appealing, ephemerally pleasurable, and in the last analysis, essentially transitory. The art of worship, it seems, moves the discussion beyond the bounds of simple aesthetic considerations, because what is mediated, revealed and celebrated in the structures of worship is none other than the divine glory, that 'terrible beauty', starkly expressed by Olivier Clément as the 'beauty of a bloodied but Resurrected face' (*Concilium*, 1980). Such stark and striking language ought at least to warn against any easy speaking of transformation. For the transformation of the Christian is nothing less than the conforming of the pattern of our own living and dying to the pattern of Christ's life and death, and this rarely occurs without the expenditure of effort and application on our part. And this introduces the often neglected dimension of *ascesis*, the indispensable discipline of a lived Christian life. *Ascesis* is a vital aspect of Christian praxis, and is essentially the practice of continually realigning oneself to the ways of God, and of recognizing that the transfiguring effect of glimpsing something of the beauty of God invariably involves a sometimes unwelcome and possibly painful reconfiguring of the pattern of our lives and loves. But this is the art of Christian living, and a chapter for a different book.

Chapter 6

Legalities, Practicalities and Other Resources

Each Church and denomination will have its own procedures and regulations concerning the reordering of churches, their furnishing and the placement of permanent works of art in the worship space. An informative guide of theological and liturgical norms and directives has been compiled and published by the American National Conference of Catholic Bishops. As might be expected, this American Roman Catholic publication, *Built of Living Stones: Art, Architecture, and Worship*, focuses upon the physical building, its design and the celebration of the sacramental rites within it, but includes some good advice on the roles of architects, builders, artists and craftsmen and how church officials might best collaborate with them.

The legalities regarding the reordering of the building and its furnishings and fittings are particularly complex and before any permanent works are done, or alterations made to a church, or its furnishings, or its churchyard, or before anything is introduced or removed from a church or chapel belonging to the Church of England, the law requires that the work be authorized by either an archdeacon's or chancellor's faculty. An archdeacon's faculty covers such things as repairs, redecoration and the introduction of minor pieces of furniture and fittings into the church which will not have a significant impact on its architectural or archaeological integrity. For all other works a chancellor's faculty is required. As a rule of thumb works such as a pulpit fall which is designed to match an existing frontal would only usually require an archdeacon's faculty (since they are minor works and do not significantly alter what is already there). However a complete new set of altar hangings in a contemporary style to be placed, say, in a medieval church are likely to require a chancellor's faculty since these would undoubtedly significantly change the feel of the existing building. Major structural works such as the replacement of a stained glass window or the insertion of a new stained glass window into the space occupied by a plain one will, too, always be subject to a chancellor's faculty.

Whenever a work is planned churches must contact the Diocesan Advisory Committee (DAC) which is the statutory advisory body in every diocese on matters affecting places of worship in the diocese. The DAC will be able to advise on which interested parties need to be consulted and involved in discussion from an early stage. These might include English Heritage and/or one of the national Amenity Societies. Each of these organizations likes to be informed of the proposed work from the start and to work with the parish and artist from inception. Indeed such consultation is required under the 2001 Faculty Jurisdiction Measure. Another benefit of working with the DAC is that most of them will have their list of those whom they consider to be competent to carry out work in various media such as stained glass, calligraphy, embroidery and textiles. Such lists do not prevent parishes from engaging other competent artists to carry out a proposed work but they do help to ensure competency of workmanship (the work of those on the list will have been tried and tested) and proven artistic ability. It is important that before a particular artist is commissioned, Church Council members or those commissioned by them look around, visiting perhaps two or three artists in their workshops or studios or going to visit their work *in situ* elsewhere before making a final decision as to which artist they wish to commission. Once a possible artist has been identified it is also important to look at other work they have done elsewhere. Since few artists now live entirely by ecclesiastical commissions, and would see confining themselves to this one sphere as almost certainly artistically debilitating, this will mean going to look at their work in a variety of different settings which might include not only the artist's own studio but also a variety of galleries and exhibitions. In the case of sculptors it might mean visiting one of the growing number of sculpture parks to look at their work. Sculpture parks in Britain and overseas are listed at www.artnut.com. This can be tremendously rewarding and educational. Few of the pieces in galleries, exhibitions or sculpture parks will be commissions and this means that one can look at work which comes from the very soul of the artist. In this way it becomes possible to understand something of what inspires the artist, what moves them and in what ways they are comfortable with handling their medium be it paint, wood, cloth or stone. This way, too, there will be a better understanding between the artist and those commissioning a work for a church when details of the commission begin to be worked out. It is also a good idea, as we have already discussed in Chapter 3, to invite the artist to come to address the PCC, or even better a church meeting, on his or her proposed design and to be willing to answer questions on the proposed work. In the case of new works it is also important to ask potential artists to submit draft designs of proposed work (perhaps first displayed at the church meeting) which are then sent to the DAC/ English Heritage and/or the appropriate Amenity Society for consultation before the final and expensive step is taken of formally commissioning the artist to draw up detailed plans and specifications.

In *Images and Idols?* Keith Walker bewails what he sees as the artistic short-sightedness of many DACs and Amenity Societies who have favoured caution, as he sees it, over all else when new works of art are under consideration in churches. This is undoubtedly sometimes true but it is also worth bearing in mind that a DAC can call upon expertise far beyond the resources of an individual parish. Though they may sometimes sound notes of caution at a proposed project, and even on occasions withhold their support, their intention is not to stop the parish from fulfilling its dream for, say, a new frontal or a new window but to prevent the parish instead from making a grievous error in matters of structural, architectural and aesthetic integrity concerning the church building which might be irreversible.

The parish must inform their church architect (usually the architect or surveyor commissioned to carry out the last quinquennial inspection) at an early stage whenever work on the church is proposed. The DAC will, in any case, need to know that this has been done and also whether the architect has any reservations about the proposed work before a DAC Certificate (Form 1) can be issued. Most dioceses require a signed declaration from the church architect before it will consider formal applications unless the architect him/herself has written the specification for the work. In some cases it will be sufficient for the parish simply to inform the architect. This safeguards the PCC and is usually without cost. However, on occasion the architect or surveyor may properly wish to ask further questions about what is proposed and may suggest a visit. Although a charge may properly be made for this it could easily save the parish money in the long run.

Once this initial consultation stage has taken place the parish needs to prepare a Statement of Significance in which the important features which contribute to the significance of the church and its history are identified and a Statement of Needs outlining why changes and additions are needed, relating to the church's worship and mission. This latter is especially significant in cases where substantial reordering is intended. The archdeacon will often be able to offer guidance as to what needs to go into the Statements of Significance and Needs. This must accompany the formal application to the DAC.

The formal application for a Form 1 (DAC Certificate), in addition to the Statement of Needs and the Statement of Significance, should also include full plans and scale drawings showing the work proposed, specifications including colour, layout material and sample lettering (where appropriate), materials (where appropriate), and drawings or photographs, illustrating the relationship of the new work with the rest of the building and not simply with its immediate surroundings. It is this area which many artists struggle with because they fear that their artistic freedom is being regulated as has already been discussed in Chapter 3. The application should also include a copy of the Parochial Church Council minute relating to the proposed work, reports on any advice which has been obtained and copies of any correspondence with English Heritage and any other relevant statutory body or Amenity Society concerned. These are then taken by the secretary to the next DAC meeting. After the proposals have been considered the DAC issues Form 1 indicating whether it has decided to recommend the proposals, to raise no objection to them or not to recommend them. Decisions on Form 1 may also have provisos attached. In the case of non-recommendation Form 1 must give the reasons for the decision. Form 1 will also indicate for the benefit of the Registrar's Office whether or not the DAC considers that the proposals will result in a significant material alteration to the appearance of the church or affect its setting and/or whether it is considered that the proposals will affect the archaeological interest of the church. This is to help the Registry determine what sort of faculty will need to be issued. Non-recommendation by a DAC only generally happens in cases where inadequate advice has been sought by the PCC before the application for a Form 1 was made, or where the DAC considers the proposed work compromises the building, its architecture, its content or its archaeology in some way. Despite how a church/PCC may feel if its proposals receive a non-recommendation at this stage DAC members are generally driven by what is best in their view for the building rather than by their own personal likes and dislikes. All decisions also do try and take into account the mission and ministry of the church making the application and the pastoral needs of that community. Often a non-recommendation at this stage can be avoided if the PCC has talked with the DAC before an artist is commissioned to draw up his or her detailed proposals and if the architect, statutory bodies or amenity societies have been consulted at an early stage. A petition may still be made to the Registrar for a faculty if the DAC has not recommended the proposal. It needs to be remembered, however, that most chancellors place considerable weight on the advice given by the DAC although they may, on occasion, override that advice if they see fit so to do.

Once a parish has obtained Form 1 from the DAC a formal application for a faculty may be made to the Registrar. The application form itself is fairly long and complex and will require research on the history of the church. The petitioners (usually the incumbent and churchwardens although it may also be the PCC) should ensure that when the application is made the wording is accurate and remains the same throughout DAC and faculty processes. If the proposal is to replace an item (such as a window) which then needs to be disposed of, both the Form 1 application and the petition should also contain a request for disposal of the item to be replaced.

At the same time as making a petition for a faculty a public notice informing the public that an application for a faculty has been made must be signed by the petitioners and published at the church. This notice, which must be displayed for a period of not less than 14 days, including a Sunday on which the church is to be used for divine worship, should also contain an address where any plans or drawings of the proposed work may be viewed. Where the church is not the parish church, the public notice should be displayed in both the church where the work is proposed and in the parish church as well. Once the public notice has been displayed for the relevant length of time it is forwarded together with a Certificate of Publication to the Registrar's Office which may then issue the relevant faculty if no objections are raised. Objections must be received within 21 days of the first publication of the public notice. Such objections tend to be a problem since no faculty can be issued until they have been resolved. Objections have tended, traditionally, to come from two different sources. The first type of objection will come from a local resident, often a non-churchgoer who would object as a matter of principle to any alterations to *their* church, however much those alterations are intended to facilitate the better performance of the worship. Sometimes it is possible to reconcile local objections by the incumbent, churchwardens or PCC chairperson approaching the individual concerned in order to explain the nature of the work proposed and the reasons for it. Faced with a direct and personal approach many such objections will, in time, disappear although patience and tact on the part of the church is often called for, often over several months! The second type of objection has often come from one of the national Amenity Societies, who by their very brief are perhaps more concerned with conservation than with mission. This is where a strong Statement of Needs relating to the church's mission may help. There is also much less likely to be an objection at this stage if the Amenity Society has been consulted from an early stage. If an objection cannot be reconciled then there is little that can be done. It is rare that a church will have either the resources or determination to appeal to the Chancellor's Court or above that to the Court of Arches (the highest court of appeal in the land in the case of ecclesiastical matters) as the vicar and churchwardens of Sherborne Abbey in Dorset successfully did during the 1990s.

A note of caution. Grant aid from English Heritage which needs to be declared in any faculty application does not only refer to a grant being sought for the current work. If aid has been given by English Heritage in the past, for example for a repair, their consent must be sought for any other repairs, alterations or new works to be done in the church even if entirely unrelated to the work for which a grant was given. English Heritage is also one of the statutory bodies which must be informed if the work proposed is likely to affect the character or special architectural or historical or archaeological interest of the church, wherever it is listed as being of Grade I or Grade II listed status.

Another category of work which may be of interest to readers is the concept of temporary reordering. If certain conditions are satisfied (such as that the work is reversible), the archdeacon can authorize temporary reordering of a church for a period of up to 15 months without a faculty to see whether the arrangements work satisfactorily and are generally acceptable. If the work is then accepted and if no further alterations are proposed a DAC Form 1 and faculty are then applied for in the normal way. The application must be made at least two months before the expiry of the existing reordering.

These arrangements of course only apply to churches and chapels in the Church of England. Non-Anglican churches all have their own procedures. For example, in the Roman Catholic Church in England and Wales there is a Committee for Church Art, Architecture and Heritage which advises the Catholic Bishops' Conference on all matters of liturgical arrangement, furnishings and fabric. Each diocese also has its own liturgical committee (and possibly also its own art and architecture sub-committee) which must be consulted whenever a Roman Catholic priest wishes to commission a work of art. The provision of vestments and altar cloths, however, is here left to the discretion of the individual parish priest who must work to the principles laid down in the *Constitution on the Sacred Liturgy*. In the Church of Scotland matters of reordering or of commissioning new works of art come under the jurisdiction of the Committee on Artistic Matters, a standing committee of the General Assembly of the Church of Scotland. It is the task of this committee to advise on all works, internal and external, which affect the appearance of a church in the care of the Church of Scotland before they happen.

Anglican cathedrals have their own unified system for consideration and authorization of works, the so-called Cathedrals Fabric Commission for England (CFCE). The Commission is a statutory body established under the Care of Cathedrals Measure (1990) to discharge specific regulatory functions and also generally to promote the care and conservation of the cathedral churches of the Church of England. The workings of this body and of how it relates to the other statutory bodies in matters of restoration and renewal have been well described by Andrew Anderson in his article 'Building and Cherishing: Cathedrals as Buildings' (Anderson, 1998).

Yet what if there is no money or no desire to introduce a permanent work of art into the local church or no desire to undertake a substantial reordering at the present time? Can no engagement then be made with the aesthetics of the liturgy or worship or with the building as a sacred space? Far from it. For many congregations who do not yet feel educated in these things there is the possibility of making one-off, temporary and experimental alterations such as moving some of the seating or chancel furniture for a special service. Such experiments need no faculty. At a training weekend for ordinands we asked a group of students and their parish support groups to 'reorder' the chapel of Sarum College, (designed by Butterfield in the mid-nineteenth century and adapted to the liturgical needs of the 1960s and 1970s) for use at the Eucharist with which we were to finish the day. Many of those who participated looked around with new eyes when given permission to experiment in this way. Most powerful perhaps was not what they brought in to the chapel but what they took out (with the promise to the college authorities that we would set all to rights at the end of the day!). In the end we were left with a room not dissimilar to a church-house of the early centuries, albeit within the constraints of a nineteenth-century Gothic revival building! And experiments of this sort need not be too ambitious. As we have seen in Chapter 5 the careful placing of the president's chair at the Eucharist can make a powerful statement too, even when done within the constraints of a medieval or Victorian building.

Another possibility is to stage a temporary exhibition of art or sculpture within the church. The possibilities here have already been described when we looked at the work of Friedhelm Mennekes and at the exhibition of sculpture staged at Salisbury Cathedral in 1999 entitled *The Shape of the Century*. Such temporary exhibitions can usefully open people's eyes to the possibility of art in churches provided no permanent damage is done to the church through hanging pictures, etc. Many local artists, some of national or international repute, may well be willing to loan their work for such a purpose. Or alternatively works may be borrowed. The Methodist Church has a clear vision for this type of interface between art and worship in its collection of contemporary Christian art which is designed to be loaned to churches. Such art, especially if it is abstract and contemporary, may well evoke strong feelings from worshippers. Yet this is often no bad thing so long as it is done sensitively. Negative responses should not always be allowed to deter us. If we are committed to giving worshippers and visitors alike an experience of the arts within worship, then we should also be willing to brave a variety of both good and bad art if our search is above all else for truth and beauty.

Resources and Addresses

Statutory and Professional Organizations, Amenity Societies and Grant-Making Bodies

Ancient Monuments Society
St Ann's Vestry Hall, 2 Church Entry, London EC4V 5HB (020 7236 3934)

Preserving former churches of historic importance through direct ownership.

British Archaeological Association
Hon. Membership Secretary, Mr J. M. Jenkins, 75 Budmouth Avenue, Weymouth, Dorset DT3 6Q J
Website at: www.britarch.ac.uk/baa

Founded in 1843 to promote the study of archaeology, art and architecture and the preservation of national antiquities. Encourages original research and publishes new work on art and antiquities from the Roman to the medieval periods. Holds an annual conference focused on the study of one of the medieval cathedrals and publishes the results of its findings in the annual Transactions of the British Archaeological Association series.

Cathedral Architects Association
46 St Mary's Street, Ely, Cambs CB7 4EY (01353 660660)

Cathedrals Fabric Commission for England
Church House, Great Smith Street, London SW1P 3NZ (Tel: 020 7898 1866; Fax: 020 7898 1881)

The Commission is a statutory body established under the Care of Cathedrals Measure 1990 to discharge specific regulatory functions and also generally to promote the care and conservation of the cathedral churches of the Church of England.

Churches Conservation Trust (formerly The Redundant Churches Fund)
89 Fleet Street, London EC4Y 1DH (020 7936 2285)

The Trust owns and looks after redundant churches of historic and archaeological interest, which have been transferred to it by the Church of England. It publishes guide books to churches in its care.

Council for British Archaeology
Bowes Morrell House, 111 Walmgate, York YO1 9WA (01904 671417)

Works to promote the safeguarding and study of Britain's historic environment, to provide a forum for archaeological research and opinion and to improve public interest in, and knowledge of, Britain's past. The CBA regularly publishes important works on the archaeology of churches.

Council for the Care of Churches
Fifth Floor, Church House, Great Smith Street, London SW1P 3NZ (Tel: 020
7898 1866; Fax: 020 7898 1881)

*A permanent Commission of the Archbishops' Council of the Church of England. The Coun-
cil's principal duty is to assist parishes in their task of maintaining their church buildings,
contents and churchyards. It publishes a wide range of specialist and general booklets on their
conservation and care, gives advice and organizes conferences. It also offers grants for the conservation of important furnishings and fittings in churches.*

Ecclesiastical Architects' and Surveyors' Association
Hon. Sec., John R. Carley, Church House, Crane Street, Salisbury, Wilts. SP1
2QB (01722 411933)

*A professional organization for church architects and surveyors which organizes lectures, and
produce technical booklets on subjects of interest to members. There is also a regular newsletter.*

English Heritage
Fortress House, 23 Savile Row, London W1S 2ET (020 7973 3000)

*English Heritage acts as an advisory body on all matters of historical and archaeological inter-
est in Grade I and II listed buildings (including churches). Includes the Royal Commission on
Historical Monuments, England which records and publishes inventories of historical monuments, including churches*

Georgian Group
6 Fitzroy Square, London W1P 6DX (020 7387 1720)

*Concerned with the study and preservation of Georgian buildings, including churches, monu-
ments, parks and gardens. Aims to save these when threatened from destruction and to
encourage appropriate repair.*

Heritage Lottery Fund
7 Holbein Place, London SW1W 8NR (020 7591 6041)

*The Heritage Lottery Fund uses money raised by the National Lottery 'to improve the quality
of life by safeguarding and enhancing the heritage of buildings, objects, and the environment . . .; assisting people to appreciate and enjoy their heritage; allowing them to hand it on
in good heart to future generations'.*

Historic Churches Preservation Trust
Fulham Palace, London SW6 6EA (020 7736 3054)

*The Trust offers grants and interest-free loans for essential fabric repairs to churches which are
in use as places of worship in England and Wales. (Grants are not offered for the restoration
of fittings or features.)*

Pilgrims Association
Secretary: Lt Colonel David Earlam, Sylvan House, Worthgate Place, Canterbury, Kent CT1 2QX (01227 454134)

The Pilgrims Association seeks to assist churches and cathedrals to meet the needs and challenges of visitors, tourists and pilgrims.

Royal Commission on the Ancient and Historical Monuments of Wales
Plas Crug, Aberystwyth, Ceredigion SY23 1NJ (01970 621200)

Established in 1908 to make an inventory of ancient and historical monuments in Wales RCAHMW carries out surveys, maintains an archive of monuments and publishes information about ancient, historical and maritime sites, structures and landscapes.

Royal Institute of British Architects
66 Portland Place, London W1B 1AD (020 7580 5533)
Website at: www.architecture.com

This is a useful springboard for links to many other sites of both historical and contemporary architectural interest including www.greatbuildings.com *which includes churches among those buildings recognized as great within both a European and a worldwide context.*

Scottish Churches Architectural Heritage Trust
15 North Bank Street, Edinburgh EH1 2LP (0131 225 8644)

The Trust gives grants to churches of special architectural or historic interest (of all denominations) to assist with repairs to the fabric of the building and its maintenance, excluding decorating and wiring. Only churches which are open for regular public worship are eligible.

Scottish Redundant Churches Trust
14 Long Row, New Lanark ML11 9DD (Tel: 01555 666023; Fax: 01555 665738)

The aims are to safeguard outstanding redundant churches of all denominations in Scotland; to maintain and protect their fabric, and to provide public access to them.

Society of Architectural Historians of Great Britain
General enquiries: Andrew Martindale, Hon. Secretary, The Society of Architectural Historians of Great Britain, 6 Fitzroy Square, London W1T 5DX

The society studies all aspects of architectural history, including churches. The website at http://www.sahgb.org.uk contains many useful links to various Amenity Societies.

Society for Church Archaeology
c/o CBA, Bowes Morrell House, 111 Walmgate, York YO1 9WA

Under the umbrella of the Council for British Archaeology the Society for Church Archaeology produces a journal and also holds an annual conference.

Society for the Protection of Ancient Buildings
37 Spital Square, London E1 6DY (020 7377 1644)

Founded by William Morris in 1877 to counteract the destructive restoration of medieval buildings, today the SPAB is the largest, oldest and most technically experienced national pressure group fighting to save old buildings from decay, demolition and damage.

Twentieth Century Society
70 Cowcross Street, London EC1M 6EJ (020 7250 3857)

Exists to safeguard the heritage of architecture and design in Britain from 1914 onwards.

United Kingdom Institute for Conservation
109 The Chandlery, 50 Westminster Bridge Road, London SE1 7QY (020 7721 8721)

Provides information and expertise on many aspects of conservation.

Victorian Society
1 Priory Gardens, Bedford Park, London W4 1TT (020 8994 1019)

Founded in 1958 the Victorian Society is responsible for the study and preservation of Victorian and Edwardian architecture and arts.

Ecumenical Links

Catholic Bishops' Conference of England and Wales: Committee for Church Art, Architecture and Heritage
Liturgy Office, 39 Eccleston Square, London SW1V 1PL (020 7901 4859)

Promotes the principles and practice of liturgical art and design and the care and conservation of Roman Catholic churches. Also acts as an advisory body to the Bishops' Conference on these matters.

Chapels Society
Honorary Secretary: Mr R. Phillips, 1 Newcastle Avenue, Beeston, Notts NG9 1BT

The Society aims to promote the survival of nonconformist places of worship and related structures throughout the UK (including those of Protestant, Catholic and non-Christian denominations and religions). It offers advice, arranges conferences and visits, supports research and publishes information.

Church of Scotland Committee on Artistic Matters
121 George Street, Edinburgh EH2 4YN (Tel: 0131 225 5722; Fax 0131 220 3113)

Offers advice and help to local churches wishing to make changes to their church building in order to 'enrich their life together or enhance their worship'. Functions as a standing committee of the General Assembly of the Church of Scotland.

Historic Chapels Trust
29 Thurloe Street, Kensington, London SW7 2LQ (020 7584 6072)

The Trust takes into ownership redundant chapels and other places of worship in England of outstanding architectural and historic interest. Anglican churches are excluded. Once in good repair, HCT's buildings are opened to the public and are available for sympathetic uses where appropriate. Local 'Committees of Friends' are being developed.

Methodist Art Collection
The Wesley and Methodist Studies Centre, Westminster Institute of Education, Oxford Brookes University, Oxford OX2 9AT

Gives information on contents of the Methodist Church Collection of Modern Christian Art and on conditions for borrowing it.

Artists Guilds and Societies

Art and Christianity Enquiry (ACE)
Director: The Revd Tom Devonshire Jones, 107 Crundale Avenue, London NW9 9PS (020 8206 2253)

Arranges seminars and conferences; promotes new works of art in churches; publishes a quarterly bulletin.

Association of Art Historians
Cowcross Court, 70 Cowcross Street, Clerkenwell, London EC1M 6EJ (020 7490 3211)

Formed in the UK in 1974 to promote the study of art history. It represents the interests of art and design historians in all aspects of the discipline including art, design, architecture and conservation.

British Society of Master Glass Painters
Secretary: Ruth Cooke, 5 Tivoli Place, Ilkley, West Yorkshire LS29 8SU (01943 602521)

Founded in 1921, this is Britain's only organization devoted exclusively to the art and craft of stained glass. It acts as both a professional society and an interest group. It produces a journal and organizes events. There is a useful website on the history and technique of stained and painted glass at www.bsmgp.org.uk.

Christian Arts (affiliated to the Secretariat International des Artistes Chrétiens)
Chairman: Gilly Seago, 14 Guildhall Street, Bury St Edmunds, Suffolk IP33 1PR (01284 754884)

A network of Christian artists, craftsmen and women, committed to exploring the use of the arts in deepening faith, and in providing a clearing house through which interested parties may contact artists with a view to exhibiting and commissioning their work. Publishes an illustrated journal three times a year.

Contemporary Art Society
17 Bloomsbury Square, London WC1A 2NG (020 7831 7311)

A charitable organization which, since its foundation in 1910, has presented over 5000 works of contemporary art to its member museums throughout Britain by artists such as Henry Moore, Francis Bacon, David Hockney, etc.

Embroiderers' Guild
Apartment 41, Hampton Court Palace, Surrey KT8 9AU (020 8943 1229)

Encourages the exchange of skills, experience and ideas through training events and publications.

Federation of British Artists
17 Carlton House Terrace, London SW1Y 5BD (020 7930 6844)

Umbrella organization which administers the following societies: Royal Institute of Painters in Watercolours, Royal Society of British Artists, Royal Institute of Oil Painters, etc. Works to educate, inspire and encourage public interest in the appreciation of fine art.

Guild of Silk Painters
Chair (2001): Mandy Southan, 69 Priory Road, Hastings TN34 3JJ

Organization for international group of silk painters from 20 different countries. There is an online journal and gallery at www.silkpainters-guild.co.uk.

Royal Academy of the Arts
Burlington House, Piccadilly, London W1J 0BD

Oldest fine arts institution in Britain (founded 1768). Website: www.royalacademy.org.uk features news, current exhibitions, etc. The library at the RA includes extensive photographic archives of all the works in the Royal Academy's permanent collections.

Society of Scottish Artists
4 Barony Street, Edinburgh EH3 6PE (0131 557 2354)

Founded in 1891 to foster an adventurous spirit in Scottish art. Aims to promote new, younger artists and to inform the public about changing ideas in modern art. They can be contacted at www.s-s-a.org.

Wales Arts International
Arts Council of Wales, Museum Place, Cardiff CF1 3NX (01222 376500)
Website at: www.wai.org.uk

Aims to give an international audience the opportunity to gain a clearer perspective on the arts from Wales.

References and Further Reading

Many of the works of art cited in this book can be viewed on the 'art and worship' page, which can be visited via the Alcuin Club website. The address is: www.alcuin.mcmail.com.

Addleshaw, G. and F. Etchells, *The Architectural Setting of Anglican Worship*, Faber and Faber, 1948.

Anderson, A., 'Building and Cherishing: Cathedrals as Buildings', in S. Platten and C. Lewis (eds), *Flagships of the Spirit: Cathedrals in Society*, Darton Longman & Todd, 1998.

Angus, M., *Modern Stained Glass in British Churches*, Mowbray, 1984.

Apostolos-Cappadona, D. (ed.), *Art, Creativity and the Sacred*, Continuum, 1996.

Aston, M., *England's Iconoclasts: Volume 1, Laws Against Images*, Oxford University Press, 1988.

Barth, K., 'The Architectural Problem of Protestant Places of Worship', in A. Bieler (ed.), *Architecture in Worship*, Oliver and Boyd, 1965.

Begbie, J., 'The Gospel, the Arts and Culture' in H. Montefiore (ed.) *The Gospel and Contemporary Culture*, Mowbray, 1992.

Begbie, J. (ed.), *Beholding the Glory: Incarnation through the Arts*, Darton Longman & Todd, 2000.

Bernstein, R., *Beyond Objectivism and Relativism: Science, Hermeneutics and Praxis*, Blackwell, 1983.

'The Bible as an Apologetic for Art', in W. D. Spencer and A. B. Spencer (eds), *God through the Looking Glass*, Paternoster Press, 1998.

Brown, D., *Tradition and Imagination: Revelation and Change*, Oxford University Press, 1999.

Brown, D., *Discipleship and Imagination*, Oxford University Press, 2000.

Brown, D. and A. Loades, *The Sense of the Sacramental: Movement and Measure in Art and Music, Place and Time*, SPCK, 1995.

Brown, F. B., *Religious Aesthetics: A Theological Study of Making and Meaning*, Macmillan, 1990.

Brueggemann, W. B., *Theology of the Old Testament: Testimony, Dispute and Advocacy*, Fortress Press, 1997.

Built of Living Stones: Art, Architecture and Worship, Guidelines of the National Conference of Catholic Bishops, US Catholic Conference, Washington DC, 2000.

Canons and Decrees of the Sacred and Ecumenical Council of Trent, trans. J. Waterworth, 1848.

Carruthers, M., *The Craft of Thought*, Cambridge University Press, 1998.

Comper, J. N., *Of the Atmosphere of a Church,* Sheldon Press, 1936.

Constitution on the Mass, 2000 VII – *Liturgical Fittings and Furnishings* Revision of the Roman Missal summarized at www.usccb.org/liturgy/current/revmissalis-romanien.htm

Couturier, Marie-Alain, *Sacred Art,* University of Texas Press, 1989.

Cranfield, N., 'Blue Heaven', *Church Times,* 1 June 2001.

Cranmer, T., *Remains,* Parker Society, 1848.

Day, M., *Modern Art in English Churches,* Mowbray, 1984.

Devonshire Jones, T., *New Art for Church Buildings,* Church House Publishing, 2001.

Dillenberger, Jane, *Style and Content in Christian Art,* SCM Press, 1986.

Dillenberger, John, *A Theology of Artistic Sensibilities,* SCM Press, 1986.

Dillenberger, John, 'Artists and Church Commissions: Rubin's *The Church at Assy* Revisited' in D. Apostolos-Cappadona, *Art, Creativity and the Sacred,* Continuum, 1996.

Doll, P., *After the Primitive Christians,* Alcuin/GROW Joint Liturgical Study 37, 1997.

Drury, J., *Painting the Word: Christian Pictures and Their Meanings,* Yale University Press, 1999.

Duby, G., *Art and Society in the Middle Ages,* Polity Press, 2000.

Duffy, E., *The Stripping of the Altars: Traditional Religion in England 1400–1580,* Yale University Press, 1992.

Eco, U., *Art and Beauty in the Middle Ages,* Yale University Press, 1986.

The Faculty Jurisdiction Rules, HMSO, 2000 (also on the web at: www.hmso.-gov.uk/si/si2000/20002047.htm).

Ford, D., *The Modern Theologians,* Blackwell, 1997.

Giles, R., *Repitching the Tent,* Canterbury Press Norwich, 2nd edn, 1999.

Guiver, G., *Pursuing the Mystery: Worship and Daily Life as Presences of God,* SPCK, 1996.

Harries, R., *Art and the Beauty of God,* Mowbray, 1993.

Hermann, B. W., 'Looking Comes First', in W. D. Spencer and A. B. Spencer (eds), *God through the Looking Glass,* Paternoster Press, 1998.

Hoche-Mong, R., 'The Artistic Dimension of Liturgy', *Studia Liturgica,* 11, 1976.

Hussey, W., *Walter Hussey Patron of Art,* Weidenfeld and Nicolson, 1985.

Irvine, C., *Worship, Church and Society,* Canterbury Press Norwich, 1993.

Irvine, C., 'A Heavenly Silence', *Expository Times,* May 2001.

Jasper, R.C.D., *George Bell,* Oxford University Press, 1967.

Kavanagh, A., *On Liturgical Theology,* Pueblo Press, 1984.

Kelly, J. 'Church Architecture: Whose End is Being Served?' *Church Building,* 60, 2000.

Lathrop, G., *Holy Things: A Liturgical Theology,* Fortress Press, 1993.

Lathrop, G., *Holy People: A Liturgical Ecclesiology,* Fortress Press, 1999.

Lewis, C., 'Transformation of Glory', in R. Harries, *Art and the Beauty of God,* Mowbray, 1993.

Loades, D., *Politics and the Nation 1450–1660,* Fontana, 1979.

Luther, M., *Works,* vol. 13, Concordia, 1958.

Luther, M., *Works*, vol. 43, Fortress Press, 1968.

Maltby, J., *Prayer Book and People in Elizabethan and Early Stuart England*, Cambridge University Press, 1998.

Milton, A., *Catholic and Reformed: The Roman and Protestant Churches in English Protestant Thought, 1600–1640*, Cambridge University Press, 1995.

Morris, W., *The Aims of Art*, Office of 'The Commonweal', 1887.

Murray, M. C., 'Art and the Early Church', *Journal of Theological Studies*, vol. XXVIII, pt 2, 1977.

Osborne, J., *Stained Glass in England*, Sutton Publishing, 1997.

Panofsky, E., *Abbot Suger on the Abbey Church of St Denis*, Princeton University Press, 1946.

Platten, S. and Lewis, C. (eds), *Flagships of the Spirit: Cathedrals in Society*, Darton Longman & Todd, 1998.

Rahner, K., 'Theology and the Arts', *Thought: Fordham University Quarterly*, 57, 1982.

Reed, Shelton J., *Glorious Battle: The Cultural Politics of Victorian Anglo-Catholicism*, Vanderbilt University Press, 1998.

Robinson, E., *The Language of Mystery*, SCM Press, 1987.

Rouet, A., *Liturgy and the Arts*, Liturgical Press, 1997.

Spencer, A. B., 'The Place of Art in Life', in W. D. Spencer and A. B. Spencer (eds), *God through the Looking Glass*, Paternoster Press, 1998.

Stancliffe, D., 'Creating Sacred Space', in D. Brown and A. Loades, *The Sense of the Sacramental: Movement and Measure in Art and Music, Place and Time*, SPCK, 1995.

Taft, R., 'How Liturgies Grow: The Evolution of the Byzantine Divine Liturgy', in *Beyond East and West: Problems in Liturgical Understanding*, The Pastoral Press, 1984.

Tillich P., *On Art and Architecture*, edited by J. and J. Dillenberger, Crossroad, 1987.

Viladesau, R., *Theological Aesthetics*, Oxford University Press, 1999.

Viladesau, R., *Theology and the Arts: Encountering God through Music, Art and Rhetoric*, Paulist Press, 2000.

Walker, K., *Images or Idols?: The Place of Sacred Art in Churches Today*, Canterbury Press Norwich, 1996.

Walker, K., 'The Mirfield Conference', *Church Times*, 6 October 2000.

Walton, J., *Art and Worship: A Vital Connection*, Liturgical Press, 1988.

Wharton, A. J., 'Ritual and Reconstructed Meaning: The Neonian Baptistry in Ravenna', *The Art Bulletin*, vol. LXIX, no. 1, 1987.

White, J. F., 'The Language of Space', *Worship*, 52, 1978.

White, S. J., *Art, Architecture, and Liturgical Reform: The Liturgical Arts Society 1920–1972*, Pueblo Press, 1990.

Wollen, D., *The Methodist Church Collection of Modern Art*, Trustees of the Methodist Church Collection, 2000.

Index

The Society for Promoting Christian Knowledge (SPCK) was founded in 1698. Its mission statement is:

To promote Christian knowledge by

- **Communicating the Christian faith in its rich diversity**
- **Helping people to understand the Christian faith and to develop their personal faith; and**
- **Equipping Christians for mission and ministry**

SPCK Worldwide serves the Church through Christian literature and communication projects in 100 countries, and provides books for those training for ministry in many parts of the developing world. This worldwide service depends upon the generosity of others and all gifts are spent wholly on ministry programmes, without deductions.

SPCK Bookshops support the life of the Christian community by making available a full range of Christian literature and other resources, providing support for those training for ministry, and assisting bookstalls and book agents throughout the UK.

SPCK Publishing produces Christian books and resources, covering a wide range of inspirational, pastoral, practical and academic subjects. Authors are drawn from many different Christian traditions, and publications aim to meet the needs of a wide variety of readers in the UK and throughout the world.

The Society does not necessarily endorse the individual views contained in its publications, but hopes they stimulate readers to think about and further develop their Christian faith.

For information about the Society, visit our website at *www.spck.org.uk*, or write to:
SPCK, Holy Trinity Church, Marylebone Road,
London NW1 4DU, United Kingdom.